Cock-Eyed Voice

Stories

Barry Grills

Books by Barry Grills

Fiction:
Cock-Eyed Voice: Stories (Fluid Grouse Enterprises)
Too Late The Hunter (Fluid Grouse Enterprises)
Oblivion (Fluid Grouse Enterprises)
I And You, And Me And Her (Fluid Grouse Enterprises)
Roadkill (Fluid Grouse Enterprises)

Non Fiction:
Every Wolf's Howl (Freehand Books)
A New Day Dawns (with Jim Brown) (Quarry Press)
Falling Into You (Quarry Press)
Ironic (Quarry Press)
Snowbird (Quarry Press)

Cock-Eyed Voice
Stories

Barry Grills

FLUID
GROUSE
enterprises

Library and Archives Canada Cataloguing in Publication

Grills, Barry, 1948-, author   Cock-Eyed Voice: Stories / Barry Grills

Cover Design: Jennifer Rouse Barbeau
Cover Photo: Jennifer Rouse Barbeau
Author Photo: Liz Lott

ISBN:
978-1-7751389-5-2

This novel is dedicated to Miss Phillips, my Grade Nine English teacher at South Carleton High School in Richmond, Ontario. Miss Phillips knew, before I did, that perhaps I should be a writer.

ACKNOWLEDGMENTS

Imagine my surprise when I began work on Cock-Eyed Voice, this collection of nearly fifty years of previously published short stories, that more than half of my stories were missing. No manuscript, no digitized version, no published magazines, all of the absent stories unavailable. In desperation, I turned to the Reference Department of Library and Archives Canada. My first heartfelt thanks must go to this vital and essential national resource. My second thank-you goes to the Reference Department which not only found the missing stories but copied them and got them to me by email. Elaine Elizabeth Radman, thank you so much. You were my human contact at the Archives on this mission and you kept on looking even when my fuzzy memory sent you down some inaccurate detours. Because of you and your help, this book is now in print.

I extend thanks as well to Quarry Magazine, Grain, NeWest Review, and the University of Windsor Review, the magazines that initially published one or more of my stories. Thanks to Oberon Press for publishing "A Game With Adonis" in its anthologies '78 *Best Canadian Stories*, edited by John Metcalf and Clark Blaise, and *Great Canadian Sports Stories*, edited by George Bowering. Thanks to Lawrence Steven for publishing "The Winning Ticket" in *Outcrops*, an anthology of short stories by Your Scrivener Press. As always, thank you to Jennifer Rouse Barbeau, who designed the cover and edited my anecdotal remarks and observations that introduce and conclude these stories. The stories did not exist in digital form when I embarked on this project and had to be re-typed from scratch. Thanks as well, then, Jennie, for going over the manuscript for typos.

CONTENTS

Behind me in the mountain pass another man
stumbles among rocks and stars
he knows about me and I know about him
we plan to get together sometime
then have a word with you

Al Purdy, *Sex & Death*

INTRODUCTION

AS I WRITE THESE FIRST FEW WORDS, it strikes me that I have been writing with uninterrupted dedication for more than fifty-five years. What will follow is a concoction of anecdotal memoir and a few short stories I published during the 1970s, 1980s and in the first decade of the new millennium. Let's face it—fifty years is half a century. I've written a great deal in that time. And a great deal has happened to the writing business during that period. Which is one of the reasons the anecdotal part is included with the stories. The anecdotes mention in passing the adversity of the writing business, what has been lost, what has been gained, and the lack of choice a writer has in getting into print what he feels the need to say. The need to write does not guarantee the economic success of writing as a profession. Every writer knows that. I've done all right, I suppose. But as a creative writer, without the buffer of journalism and other jobs that came my way, I would have starved to death years ago.

The second reason for the anecdotal part of this short volume is that I met some interesting people along the way. And fifty years of published writing means fifty years of editors, publishers and other writers, all of whom had a role in the changing nature of how writing got published then or gets published now. And many of them, as well as the times, had an impact on me as a writer. There's some history in the subject, you see.

Ah yes, the history. The writing process probably hasn't changed much, historically speaking, but getting it into print has changed a great deal. My introductions to the stories in this volume offer not only a personal and historic view of how the writing business has changed, but also bear witness to human characteristics. We each participate in our cultural collective; perhaps my musings might even reflect some idea of what lies ahead. Us old guys, us old writers, are elders in the writing tribe. What we've been through, I hope, has something valuable to say. Imagine us, writers and readers, sitting down to dinner. I'm just passing the potatoes without you having to ask for them. You can say, "no thank you" if you want and do without or accept the small scoop that's offered.

A WORD ABOUT HOW IT ALL BEGAN. Grade Nine, South Carleton High School in Richmond, Ontario, a small town near Ottawa back then. Couldn't have cared less about writing. I was a reader, I admit, frequent, even relatively avid. But football, baseball, other athletics, these were where my interests lay.

At some point during my freshman year in high school—I don't remember the season—my parents dutifully went to parent-teacher interviews at my school. They brought home one surprising comment from my slate of teachers that year. My English teacher—Miss Phillips, I recall—told them that I, their not very scholastic and not all that literate son, should perhaps be a writer. How she came by this prognosis I will never know. My parents passed on this news in the same good-humored dismay that I received it. Writer? What? I soon forgot about this unexpected observation, especially once my family moved to Belleville, Ontario, that summer and I left South Carleton High School behind, presumably along with any dubious suggestion I might be an author.

But there were English classes in Grade Ten at Moira Secondary School too. And one assignment that year was to write a short story. I dutifully did my homework every night—most of us did in those days— and this included my short story, something about a group of soldiers in a foxhole who were dealing with the fact they were going to die. In short, it was introspective and philosophical. At fifteen, I had discovered that introspection and ideas excited me much more than bullets, guns, heroes and carnage. I had no typewriter; I wrote this story longhand. I do not remember its title. I do know, though, that I received a near-perfect mark and that I wanted to write more stories. In my spare time. On the weekends. After school. At night, when I could have been watching more television. Miss Phillips in Grade Nine would have been redeemed, had she known. She thought I should be a writer. Lo and behold, approximately a year later, I wanted to be a writer. Badly, endlessly, desperately. All the bloody time!

Let me explain a distinction. What I really mean is that I wanted—badly, endlessly, desperately—to write. I wanted to tell stories. I wanted to be, in a creative way, in a state of perpetual argument with the conventional mores of society. I couldn't help myself. It was crazy. I just had to do it. The other side of the coin, a contrary distinction, is wanting to be a writer. I understand anyone who tells me they want sincerely to write—we are comrades in arms. But tell me you want to be a writer, well, I wonder why you want to make no money, have most of your friends and family not read what you write, endure endless rejection and misunderstanding, run a gauntlet of rules that rarely make sense, and be considered some kind of introverted lunatic who should get a real job. Who would want a career defined by such inadequate rewards?

There is a point at which the circle of needing to write and the circle of becoming a writer overlap. The area of intersection is publishing: you must publish your writing to have three square meals a day so that you can keep writing. People must read your writing so that they can want to read some more of what you write—this too is accomplished through publishing. And when the need to write is strong enough, all those challenges that make being a writer very tough are somehow worth it. I can truthfully say I have never regretted wanting to write. I have regretted numerous times, however, wanting to be a writer, despite the times it has been rewarding.

I ENCOUNTERED ACCIDENTALLY A LARGE TOME dedicated to the writing business at the public library, when I was sixteen or so. It was called *Writer's Digest,* a voluminous, annually-updated list of places to send short stories, articles, novels, plays and every other written work for publication. I borrowed this book from the library, renewed it as often as I could and then eventually saved my money and purchased my own current version. It went with me everywhere. As I sat in the back seat of the car on road trips, this book was open in my lap. I read it in bed, I took it to school, and I still read the borrowed version at the library even as I was turning it in.

Not only did it have market information—the places to sell your work—but articles about how to do it properly. Editors, the book reported, would encourage you if they thought you had promise. The emphasis, though, was on getting your work to the place likely to accept it, a complicated business. If you refined your craft and sent your work to the right publication in a professional way, you would ultimately get published and be on your way. The articles cautioned young writers such as me that developing your craft could take many years, depending on your progress and knowledge about where to send your work. The articles also advised writers to let their own voice evolve. They warned against copying the writing styles of writers whose work we loved or admired. Find your own voice, they said. In other words, be honest as a writer. As a former teacher of the art of public speaking, I used to advise, "love yourself, love your material and love your audience." Writing is similar to public speaking, in my opinion, though in a large, abstract way. Believe in yourself, write with honesty and embrace any audience that appreciates the first two points in the formula.

Everything *Writer's Digest* said was true back in my youth. I began to develop my own voice. I wrote short stories. I carefully prepared them to be sent out to magazines that, in their listings, explained what they were looking for. I met the rejection slip. I met more rejection slips. They swarmed me. I wrote more stories. I sent them out. More swarms of rejection slips. Then . . . personal letters of encouragement. From magazines in New York (what were then termed "the slicks"). Some of these letters, no doubt dictated and always personally signed, offered advice along with a good deal of encouragement, sometimes a page and a half of it. These letters almost always closed with an invitation to send them something else. Forty or fifty years ago, publishers had policies in place to encourage writers and wise, skillful editors did so on their behalf. People, not bots. A far cry from today's "if you don't hear from us, we don't want it" responses to submissions.

Writer's Digest not only listed the high-paying slick magazines but the university and literary presses, and as I found my voice, I eventually realized that the literary magazines were the market to which I should send my stories. These were the publications made for my writing *voice*.

AND NOW TO THE TITLE of this amalgam of brief memoir and humble collection: *Cock-Eyed Voice: Stories.* Oblivious to my potential sensibilities, an editor once grudgingly accepted one of the stories in this book with a lament that he was taking it despite my "cock-eyed voice." I let it go. Now many years later, I have come to believe I do, indeed, have a cock-eyed writing voice. But cock-eyed or not, it's *my* voice and it reflects *my* version of the truth. Short stories, I think, should do more than entertain. They should make the reader squirm. With regard to theme, I'm invested in showing interior lives, whether they might be perceived as politically correct or not. We live our lives in three different persons and tenses. That's at the root of my writing voice. I like to display all the persons and tenses in both long and short work, the "I", "you", and "he/she/they" elements we all experience personally. Cock-eyed, I guess. And there's that squirming thing I mentioned.

So be it.

A note about grammar, style and editing. Because this small collection represents a fairly long historical period, I am maintaining the grammar and style—indeed some of the weak verbs, for example—that editors retained in the days when the original stories were published. Style and grammar can then appear "on the record" too. I see an evolution in these stories and perhaps you, the reader will too.

At some point at the end of the eighties I discovered that the short story and I were no longer interested in one another, which is part of why this collection is so short. Eventually I discovered short stories were fodder for novels for me, and I preferred to apply my cock-eyed voice to the novel form.

So here are my stories as they appeared over the past five decades. Warts and all.

TALENT

My first published short story appeared in Quarry Magazine *in the autumn of 1973. W.J. Barnes was the editor at the time and David Helwig—whom I would know in later years through various interactions in* The Writers' Union of Canada—*was the book review editor. Among the other prose notables in this issue of* Quarry *were Matt Cohen and John Newlove.*

TALENT, the story that follows, had been accepted more than a year earlier and I had despaired that it would ever actually come out. But it finally did. I put the issue of Quarry *on the coffee table of the small apartment I shared with my wife, frequently reading the other offerings in the magazine, but often merely glancing at it and feeling a wondrous sense of achievement. It felt like redemption. By this time I had gained four years' experience as a daily newspaper reporter, beginning when I was eighteen. In the newspaper sense, seeing my byline in print was essentially already ordinary. But* Talent *was my first published piece of creative fiction; it was special.*

The magazine languished on the coffee table for many months. No one in my circle read it. People "out there" did because, in the years that were the 1970s, writers would receive infrequent letters of appreciation for their work from readers. I too would get such letters for Talent *and other stories. Back then, a great deal of appreciation was expressed in a note for the cost of a postage stamp.*

TALENT

I HEAR COOPER, THE FOREMAN, calling Steve to lunch and I know he will come to find me next. Quickly, I dip the roller into the tray and push it back and forth with the long handle until it is soaked. The paint is beige. I have grown to accept its monotony as I have grown to accept all the monotonous things about this apartment building. I turn the roller towards the wall and spread the color on the plaster that has been put there just a couple of days before. I like the foreman to see me working hard when he comes to tell me it's lunch time or when he comes to check on my work or tell me it's quitting time.

"Time for lunch," he says, standing in the doorway not far from where I work.

"Okay," I say, stroking the wall a few more times, being careful not to leave a streak.

He watches me as I pour the remaining paint in my tray into a paint can in a corner of the room. As I turn around, he tosses me my lunch in a paper bag. I drop it. He turns away down the hall as I pick it up.

Cooper drives me to work in the mornings and then takes me home at quitting time because we live on the same block. He is a friend of my father's and that is why I have this job for the summer. I'm not supposed to work until I'm sixteen, but I'm big for my age and look older so I can work a year early. My father wanted me to have this job. He thinks I should be responsible.

I follow Cooper down the long hall that separates the various apartments. At the end of the hall he enters a doorway. That is the apartment he has selected today in which we will eat our lunch. He likes us to eat together. Although I don't really understand why, I suppose it is because he is the boss and wants to be the boss even when we are eating.

This is my second week on this job. Steve started this week. He and I are painting the undercoat and we are on the third floor. Cooper is working one floor below, putting on the glossy coat. He is working alone because his helper has phoned in sick. Steve started this week because Cooper's other man suddenly quit.

The apartment building is twelve storeys high and I often think I will quit before we make the top. There are still nine floors left and I am bored with the same color of the paint and the same shape of the rooms. I am bored that each floor has the same number of apartments and each apartment has the same number of rooms.

And I don't like the sloppiness in the building. There

are lengths of wood scattered on the floor here and there. Some are in piles along the walls. There are hard masses of plaster where the plasterers have slopped and not bothered to clean up their mess. The plasterers are on the fifth floor now and we try to stay two floors behind them.

Apartment buildings like this one are going up all over the city and this one was started in the spring. It stands in one of the city's older sections. Old houses still remain on each side of the apartment and eventually they will be torn down so that new apartments may be built. More houses of the same type are located on the other side of the street.

This is the Italian community and I have never seen Italian communities before coming to this job. They appear just the way I expected them. I used to listen to my father talk about the mess in this part of the city. There's always washing hanging on the line just like you'd expect. The grass is always torn up on their lawns and their yards are often littered with toys or garbage. Just what you'd expect, I guess.

But it's hot. Everything looks worse when it's hot. The first day on the job wasn't too bad. It was cooler then. Now it's very hot. Since the second day on the job the temperature has been in the high eighties and low nineties every day and I've seen all the workers sweating. I sweat a lot myself, but if the plaster is fresh it seems cooler in the rooms. It's always hot in July. You can't stop work just because it's hot, my father said when he thought I was griping. I wasn't griping. It's just hot work.

In the room that Cooper has selected he is sitting down with Steve and opening his lunch. We eat on the balconies that have been built on the end of each room. There we can look out over the street and catch anything that might be going on. The balconies are very cool to sit on and, at noon, the sun doesn't shine on us because the balcony on the next floor shields us.

I sit down, unwrap a sandwich and start to eat. The first week I didn't mind eating sandwiches every day. This week I have grown tired of them and sometimes I have to force them down. My mother has mentioned that she will put soup in a thermos for me, but I told her not to bother because it would be too much trouble. She works very hard at home.

None of us talk while we eat. Instead we just look out from the balcony across the street or onto the street where we can watch cars go by. We all think about something. I am not thinking about anything important. It's hard to begin talking when you've been painting alone all morning and only had your thoughts for company. When I go home after work, I don't talk much because I am enjoying what I'm thinking about. It's very comfortable and honest, more honest than saying things just for the sake of saying them.

Sometimes though, Steve and I get talking. Cooper starts us at opposite ends of a floor and we work towards one another. After awhile we meet in the middle apartment. Then we start talking. I like talking to Steve most of the time although he is very serious about everything. He has a lot of gripes with the world. There are many things he doesn't like to do and he talks a lot about going to Europe and bumming around. I have never heard him laugh happily. He laughs a little when he says something critical about something, but it is a very sad laugh. I don't think he has a sense of humor. I like to laugh sometimes when the mood hits me. But there's no joking with Steve. Sometimes I don't think he's very happy with himself.

Steve was hired to work on the building as a construction worker. But his foreman transferred him to Cooper when Cooper's other painter quit. Steve doesn't care. It's just a summer job. He goes to university where he says he is taking English and philosophy. He doesn't know what he is going to do after school although he writes poetry in his spare time. He is only five years older than I am, but he worries a lot more. He talks a lot about smoking grass and hash and he acts superior to me when he talks about it. I don't care about his acting superior. I've tried smoking it once and it wasn't anything special. But Steve's a fanatic about it. Everybody should smoke pot, Steve says, just to be a human being. I don't mind.

Steve has a helluva great moustache. I think he strokes it when he is by himself. I've seen him reach up to stroke it and then stop himself because I was looking at him. It's a great moustache. Really thick.

I don't like Cooper very much. In a way, he frightens me. He seems to be very stupid. Cooper has six children and, when he and his family visit my parents, he ignores the kids completely, even when the small ones start punching him. His wife disciplines the kids. But, somehow, I can tell he has a severe temper. He drinks a lot of beer. I've seen him sitting in the yard in front of his house, wearing just a T-shirt when it's hot, drinking bottle after bottle. He has a beer belly. His face is very fat too. He looks fatter because he is very bald. His eyes are sunk in between the mounds of fat on his cheekbones and they squint out at you like lights in tiny windows.

I don't like looking at him when he eats. He smacks and makes other noises and the sandwiches stick to the roof of his mouth. When he eats, you can see all the food in his mouth. I don't like it but I always seem to accidentally look at him when he is eating. After he finishes he burps for a long time and never excuses himself. My mother doesn't like it either.

We eat without talking. Below us, the cars pass and stir up the dust on the street and I think about how angry the women must be when they bring their washing in and find it all soiled with the dirt from this building. Cooper sweats around the edge of his painting cap.

Two Italian workers come out on the balcony only a few yards away from us. They unwrap their sandwiches and start to eat. Their sandwiches are huge, made with large pieces of bread. The bread looks homemade and I would like to swap sandwiches with them just to see if they are better than mine. I don't understand why the Italians are eating on this floor. They are plasterers and they are two floors above us. I notice that Cooper and Steve are wondering the same thing. I want to stop staring at them for I have seen them before. But I can't.

I recognize one of the Italians. He is very tall and doesn't have a shirt on. He looks like an ape. His hair sticks out from his body, black and thick. I remember him from a week before on the first or second floor. He pissed on a wall I had just painted. The plumbing on the first floor wasn't hooked up then and we were supposed to piss in the back yard behind some trucks. But he pissed on the wall. I should have repainted it because it stained it a little. But I couldn't do it. I couldn't paint a wall that someone had pissed on.

I don't know the other one. He is a lot smaller and very handsome. Most of the Italians I have seen are quite handsome. When they are young. He has long dark hair and it is cut well. He does most of the talking. The big one just laughs at what he says. I can't understand what they are saying, but I know they are having a lot of fun. We must look strange to them, just sitting there and eating our sandwiches without saying anything.

I finish my lunch and drop the wax paper into the bag. I sip the pop that Cooper and I have stopped for early in the morning on our way to work. I watch Steve stretch and then move closer to the edge of the balcony and put his legs between the railings. He lets them dangle there. I think it must be uncomfortable. Cooper leans back against the wall and closes his eyes. It is quite cool on the balcony so far, but it will get hotter in a couple of hours.

I close my eyes too.

I feel someone hit me on the leg and I open my eyes again. Steve looks at me and then gestures towards the street. I move closer to the edge of the balcony.

Steve whistles softly. "Look at that," he says.

At first I don't know what he wants me to see. Then I notice a girl walking along the other side of the street.

"Just look at that chick, will ya," Steve says.

It is strange to see Steve so impressed. When we talk, he never questions anything about girls. I watch her because I am curious.

At first she is too far away to be seen clearly and I wonder how Steve has been able to judge her. But she moves closer now, walking quickly down the street, a handbag swinging from a strap in her hand.

She is Italian and very beautiful. I can tell this now that she is closer. She has very big breasts and they bounce as she walks. I like her clothing and the way it fits so well. She has a miniskirt and very fine legs. I don't think she is wearing anything under her blouse because her breasts sag a little with their own weight. Her black hair is shining in the sunlight and it has a July haze about it, as if she should be on the beach. I am fascinated by the jelly movement of her breasts. She is beautiful in her big sunglasses. She stops at the bus stop just in front of where we sit, but she is far away on the other side of the street.

I feel conscious of everything around me. As the girl stands by the bus stop post, perhaps looking up at us, I am more sensitive to what is around me. The Italians have stopped talking and have been watching her too, but now they start their jabbering again. They are laughing about something again. Cooper has been watching too. Now he leans back and I turn to see him close his eyes again. I hear Steve sigh. He looks at me for a moment. He has a helpless look on his face.

"Did you see those boobs?" He does not look at me as he asks. He is staring at the girl again. "I can't stand it," he says. He turns from the railing, painfully pulling his legs rom the openings, and turns his back on the girl. He rests against the iron work.

"What's wrong?" I ask him after he is quiet for a long time.

He rests his head in his hands and looks at his feet. "Girls like that. I've never had a girl like that."

"Me neither," I say.

He doesn't look up from his boots. "Just look at her. Can you imagine squeezing those boobs?"

I don't know if I can imagine that. I have never squeezed any before.

Steve looks at me, but I don't think he is waiting for an answer.

"All my life I've wanted girls like that and never had any." He shrugs hopelessly.

"Maybe you will someday," I say.

"Sure," Steve says, but he is still very sad.

I don't know what to say right now so I look at the girl again. I guess she is very beautiful. But Steve is making too much out of her. She turns sideways for a moment. Her breasts are big. She reminds me of Cynthia, at school.

I love Cynthia. At school I feel embarrassed when I see her. I stare at her all the time. She is in my class and she is very beautiful too. The girl at the bus stop reminds me of Cynthia, but she is different. Cynthia is my age. Too young. Her breasts are nice, I suppose, but not as big as the Italian girl's. I think Cynthia is more beautiful. I haven't seen her since school closed and twice this summer I missed her so much I almost started to cry. During the whole school year I loved her. When she was sick and didn't come to school, I felt very bad. I just liked to look at her. I don't think about touching her except when I am home in bed. Then I kiss her very softly. I don't think about having her the way Steve means. I just like to remember the way she moved her head and the way she smiles sometimes. I like to pretend I am kissing her. But I don't want to have her the way Steve means. I wouldn't say anything to anyone. I'd be embarrassed.

When I first knew I loved Cynthia, I thought it would be easy for her to love me. I wouldn't have to say anything to her. It would just happen. When I was younger, I thought it would be easy for anyone to love me. Now I know it is hard most of the time. If it was easy, Cynthia would love me. What I don't understand is how it was so simple for me to love her. She finds it easier to be with the guys who are older and have cars. I don't really think it's love with those guys. But I don't think she would let herself love me.

I think about her too much. I stop myself. Steve is talking to me again and I listen so I will not think about her.

"I have a dream," Steve is saying. "In this dream I'm in a long hall at the university. I seem to be alone at first, but then I notice a bunch of doorways leading into the hall. A girl at the university, as gorgeous as the one down there, keeps walking towards me in the hall. I notice some guys in the other doorways, standing there without moving, watching this beautiful girl walk up the hall. I'm standing in a doorway too. The girl stops and looks over the guys in each doorway and then she moves on. I wait a long time while she looks over the other guys and then she stops in front of me and looks me over. Jeezus, is she beautiful. Then she smiles at me and leans up and kisses me and it's the most fantastic kiss I've ever imagined. She hasn't kissed any of the others so I guess I've won her or something. Then I wake up and it's morning."

There is silence. Steve looks up at me from his boots.

"How's that for being neurotic? That's what it's like to be really screwed up about something."

"I have dreams too," I say.

"So we're both screwed up," Steve says. "Even if the dream came true, the kiss wouldn't be like that. I've kissed girls. You come to expect bad breath. But the kiss in the dream is like spring flowers. How do you explain it?"

"I don't know," I say.

Steve turns around again to stare down where the girl has been standing. I stretch to see if she is still there and, when I learn she is, I relax again. I turn to look at

Cooper. His eyes are still closed. He is probably asleep. I look at Steve again. I feel I should say something.

"She's just a girl," I say. My voice scares me when I hear it after the silence. I think I have said something bad.

He turns to me and shows his cynical smile. "You're very young, aren't you?"

I scowl at him. I don't know what to say. I see Steve look at the girl again and his words have made me feel ashamed of myself.

"Someday it'll happen to you," Steve says without looking at me. "You'll see some chick walk down the street like that and you'll wonder who's had her and why it wasn't you."

I nod, but I haven't been listening. I think Steve is being silly. I think of Cynthia again. Cynthia is not just a girl. I am not so young. She is the girl I love. Cynthia is a person. The girl by the bus stop is just a girl. I know Cynthia. I do not know the girl by the bus stop.

"You don't even know who she is," I say.

The Italians have stopped talking again and I know they are listening to us. I do not look at them.

"I know what I like," Steve says.

It is a stupid thing to say. I don't think Steve knows what he likes. He just knows what he wants. I think there is a difference.

"I'd have to know her name," I say, "before I could care about her."

"That's your hang-up."

"She probably has the bad breath you were talking

about," I say because I am peeved. "We all do most of the time."

"If we got together, it wouldn't matter," Steve says. He doesn't stop looking at the girl. "I'd spend most of my time with those boobs."

"Boobs aren't everything," I argue. "I'd want her to like me. I'd have to care about her. I'd want to know her name first."

Steve pays no attention to me. Instead, beside me, I notice Cooper moving. He opens his eyes and then closes them again. Now he opens them and leaves them open. He rubs them. He has been sleeping.

"Her name is Rosa," the handsome Italian says from the other balcony.

I look at him and he is grinning. The hairy one is looking at us stupidly. I don't think he speaks English. The handsome one turns his grin on Steve.

"I have made love with her," he says. "I can tell you about it because you are very curious. She bites her lip all the time when she is making love. And she curls her toes. I have felt them tickling my feet. I have made love with her three times."

I look at Steve and he is very pale in the shadow of the balcony.

Cooper has been watching Steve and suddenly he laughs loudly and I feel like laughing too. I stop myself. I watch Cooper slap his leg and laugh louder. It is difficult for me not to laugh.

Steve looks very angry. "Bullshit," he says to the Italian. But his voice is very weak.

Cooper stops laughing as suddenly as he began.

The Italian shrugs. "It doesn't matter, but I will show you."

He stands up by the railing and leans over it a little.

"Hey, Rosa," he shouts. He waves his arm. "Hey, Rosa, up here."

All of us watch the girl. She shields her eyes for a moment and then appears to smile. She waves to the handsome Italian. They wave at one another continuously for a few seconds. Finally, he blows her a kiss and she returns it. The bus comes and we can no longer see her.

The Italian sits down. "Ah, well," he says. "You see?"

Steve is not looking now. He picks up his lunch bag and whips it over the balcony. He walks quickly by me, heading back to work.

Cooper laughs again.

The Italian watches Steve leave and then grins at me. He shrugs.

I smile back because I am embarrassed.

Cooper stands up. "Back to work," he says.

I nod and get to my feet. I look at the Italian again and he is still grinning at us.

His teeth are very white.

I am just glad he has not had Cynthia.

DEATH BY SENIORITY

The issue of Quarry Magazine *in which* Talent *appeared had announced on its masthead page that, due to a high volume of material, it would not be considering any other submissions for approximately a year. I cannot remember if my next story to be published by* Quarry *was already written or if I wrote it afterwards. Certainly, I thought if* Quarry *would publish one of my stories they would likely consider another one. They did, and they did.*

This time, the spring issue 1976 even had my name on the cover with five other authors and poets. Barry W. Grills. I can no longer remember what compelled me to include my middle initial in the early days, but at some point I dropped it. As I write this introduction now, I am strangely relieved that I did. The middle initial seems pretentious to me now.

My most satisfying anecdote about the publication of this story surrounds Al Purdy. Although there were long gaps between our meetings, I had already met the great poet on two other occasions, interviewing him for the local Belleville newspaper, The Intelligencer. On the second occasion, he had invited me to a reading he was doing at Belleville Collegiate Institute and Vocational School a day or so hence. I attended at his invitation. But that's another story.

On the day that the story which follows, DEATH BY SENIORITY, showed up in my mailbox in published form, a small writers group to which I belonged had arranged a visit to Mr. Purdy's cottage—now a heritage literary site—in Prince Edward Country on Roblin Lake. Al Purdy was always interested in new writers and often welcomed them to his home, a tradition that continues at the heritage site where writers in residence come to work and greet other visitors today.

I remember a few things about this visit: that the great poet was watching the CFL game on television inside when we arrived; that we all met together around a campfire for our discussions; that he read one of his poems to us—making a point about romantic love raised in our conversation—that he snatched from his typewriter somewhere inside his cottage; and that he was genuinely pleased when one of my companions told him I'd had my second short story appear that day in Quarry. He told me Quarry was a very good magazine. I recall telling him the title.

As for the unforgettable poem he read that night? It was Subject/Object, which later appeared in his *collection,* Sundance At Dusk.

DEATH BY SENIORITY

I DIDN'T LIKE YOU, ERIC. From the very first day. Although it seemed we were friends, I couldn't like you because of the type of man you were. Dislike can develop into hatred. So be it. I've learned, in many respects, to hate you. For the thing you did I never expected, but should have expected.

I've met other people like you and felt ashamed of them, people from whom things are taken and never returned. Like wolves, they bow in disgrace before the pack leader, graciously accepting every cuff or snarl as their due.

That was you, Eric. You had no strength, no survival instinct, no will to win. You had no bestial sense of the human jungle. People took from you, but you never took from them. They bullied you, but you never bullied back. You never found the seniority required to live in the jungle. You were the smallest, most defenseless animal on the veldt, a wingless bird or a legless impala among the lions.

I knew it that first day in April when you walked into the garage out of the rain, looking so out of place and timid. I could sense you were a victim. It was in your short, slender frame and your fidgeting, twitching mannerisms. I saw the premature wrinkles of worry around your youthful eyes, the trembling uncertainty of your alto voice.

You were twenty-five years old. Yet, you looked older in a victimized way, as if you had seen eighty years of your own misery. At the same time, you looked younger, as if those eighty years had taught you nothing.

You were obviously overwhelmed by the big, looming buses that were more at home in the garage. It was as if you stood at the base of some great monument. You were reverent, frightened by the fearsome mystery, strength and force of the colossal structures around you. Their imposing solidarity threatened your frail mortality. In the garage, sometimes, it seems the metal muscle of the buses will outlast the delicate pulse of humanity by decades. I know it seemed that way to you.

You met the mechanics whose knowledge of the intimate vibrations of the machinery has turned them into hardened, predatory giants. You met the other drivers who have learned to leash and finally command the big, metallic monsters, we who have learned to endure and be strong. You said you were glad to know us, but we were aware of the limp hesitation and fearful apprehension in your handshake.

We began, in turn, to try to teach you the mystery of the machinery. We tried to explain the secrets that would enable you to conquer the gladiatorial vehicles, make them do your bidding. You shrank back and learned slowly, already awed by the overpowering strength in others that you would never possess.

Selfishly, I knew you were to be my victim. Before you, I had no seniority. All the tedious, unwanted chores were mine. The busiest, most difficult routes. The last choice of vacation. Worst of all, from November to May, I had endured the hated night shift which, in the end, was the ultimate test for any new driver. Those who failed and sought employment elsewhere were generally those who could not conquer the eerie nightmare of the night shift.

All of us, the other drivers, had seen weak men come and go. Yours was the most obviously predestined failure we had ever encountered. You were as out of place as snow in July. We didn't know why you were learning to drive instead of in a shoe store, selling gentle footwear to gentle ladies on gentle Monday mornings.

You told me one night that you didn't have any choice. We were driving the same shift and taking a coffee break in a downtown restaurant.

"I have to drive," you said.

The coffee was scalding, but we gulped it down. You hadn't learned yet to accept hurried hot drinks as a way of life.

"I've had quite a few jobs," you said, talking too slowly for the amount of time left.

"Me too," I said.

"Hell," you said with regret. "I've even been in the insurance business. I had to quit that because I took 'no' for an answer. I didn't make any money. No matter what I've done, I've never really succeeded."

You looked at me in search of sympathy. "You know how rough it is to get a job these days."

"Yeah. It's rough."

"Well, I applied for this job and I got it. I have to have work, just like everybody else. I have a wife and a little girl. Driving bus pays pretty good, I suppose. I've worked for a lot less."

"Yeah. It's not bad," I said.

"Anyway, here I am."

You were pathetic to me. Sympathy embarrasses me because I don't like its weakness. I was harsh with you.

"We all have to do things," I said. "You're not special."

"Oh, I know," you replied quickly. "I didn't mean it to sound like self-pity."

"You have to learn like everybody else," I added, despising the note of apology in your voice.

You were quiet, so easily beaten.

"You have to be tough. Hard. You have to look out for number one. Everybody's against you, one way or another. The drivers have seniority over you. They'll bump you into all the crap they can because they don't want it. They're looking out for number one, you see. If they weren't they'd take the bad shifts themselves, wouldn't they? But they bump you into it instead, because you don't matter."

I watched you for a moment. "Just like I'm going to bump you in November."

You shrugged, unable to look at me.

"And the passengers," I said. "They'll report you if you so much as breathe the wrong way. They're out to get your job. You have to remember, when you're driving, you're nothing but a machine, nothing more than the steering wheel or the transmission. You're not a person, just another nut and bolt. No one cares about you. The sooner you accept that, the better it is for you."

"You're very bitter," you said.

"Nah. I'm a realist."

I saw you watching the other drivers the first few months. I knew they mystified you because they were distorted human beings, misshapen with their round shoulders warped from so much wrestling with the wheel. They looked like apes, strong arms and weak legs. Their stomachs were puffy from thousands of hours in the same seat. Their backs were weakened from carrying too much excess weight and too little hope. You watched them, feeling sorry and disgruntled. You saw yourself among them and it frightened you. Already you wanted out, after only a few months. Yet, you stayed because you were waiting for seniority and you needed the job. Already, your future had run out of possibilities. You were locked into your situation as inexorably as us all.

Summer came. A rivulet of sweat. I took my holidays along with the other drivers, but you kept going. You hadn't earned a vacation yet. At night, you were harassed by drunks. In the afternoon, you waged war with the traffic, losing most skirmishes because you weren't an aggressive driver. You had difficulty maintaining schedule because the other vehicles bullied position away from you.

I don't know why, but I tried to help you, even though you made me angry. I resisted my sympathy but it was there just the same.

"Don't let cars push you around," I said. "You have a schedule, they don't. You're bigger than they are. When it comes down to a showdown, you'll win every time. You have to be tough and mean in traffic. They'll beat you if you don't."

You nodded in understanding.

"Losing in traffic," I said, "is like losing in everything else. Pointless as hell."

You studied me for a moment. "Sometimes losing is winning," you said.

I shrugged, then spat on the pavement.

"Crap," I muttered.

You continued to falter in traffic. The passengers frayed your nerves. You made me angry because you didn't fight back. I expected you to quit anytime because I knew you were going to fail. Yet, you kept going through the sweaty summer and into the fall.

You thought we were friends because I tried to help you, because I let you buy me a beer now and then. You couldn't see that I disliked you. You didn't suspect that you represented, in every way, the kind of man I despise—weak and unimposing, a sucker, an ineffectual fish out of water, a loser. I let you buy the beers because you wanted to and I had, to some extent, given up on you. I was sure it was only a matter of time until I wouldn't have to put up with you anymore.

I went around to your apartment where, in your own domain, you were an even greater mystery to me. I sat in your tiny living room among a multitude of books, records, empty wine bottles and candles. Your simple possessions were, to me, nothing more than the world's stormy confusion. You forced me to borrow books I had never heard of before which I never found time to read. You wanted me to listen to your records, but I complained that it was noise.

I came back because of your wife, not you. She wore no bra and very short skirts, and she wanted me to sleep with her. I didn't like her very much either, Eric. Your brazen, seductive wife. I didn't like the way she criticized you and ordered you about as if you were a servant. I hated you for allowing it or, at least, allowing me to see it.

Yet, I went back to your place again and again, hoping to see you fight back. It never happened. Or I went back, sometimes, to look at your wife, to be seduced by her. I cursed you for not noticing. I went back because you were a victim and I was a predator. Our continued companionship emphasized that fact.

I made love to your vampire wife, Eric, one September afternoon. I bullied her as she bullied you, but she was invincible. She didn't care about you or me or anyone else. In your bed, she and I were prey and predator alike.

November and the night shift came. Without a compassionate thought, I bumped you from your run and forced it upon you as if it were some punishment you had earned. I thought it would make you quit.

At the end of November you entered the ethereal

world of the night shift. I knew how it would be for you, because it had been that way for me. You swept up candy wrappers, potato chip bags, germ-filled tissues and hundreds of empty popcorn boxes. You carried out the garbage and washed the buses every night, the power spray fighting you every second until you thought your muscles would fail. You shoveled wheelbarrows of mud from the wash bay only to have it accumulate again a night or two later. I know. I did it too.

Every night you were left alone in the creaking conversation of the garage with its banging, clanging heating pipes, its roaring boiler and whispering walls. Alone, you learned the building's hoarse secrets—the shadows in the corners, the darkness behind the buses and terrifying snap of the vehicles as they settled. Outside, in the yard, where the waiting monsters idled, you heard noises that seemed demonic when they were actually nothing more than the protesting moans of machinery. You jumped in terror when you passed your own reflection in a window or mirror. You listened breathlessly when you heard the relentless sigh of the wind or the invective hiss of the rain on the roof. You jumped when snow fell from the wheels with a sudden, maddening plop. One by one, these frightening sounds made you frantic.

Alone, your thoughts cascaded and tumbled like streams and geysers. The things you once imagined became certainties and the certainties you had known became imaginings. Your spirit began to break down like eroding soil along the bank of a river. Sometimes, in the bathroom, you vomited because food wouldn't stay down anymore.

The night shift created nightmares you had never had before. Coils of electric wiring and swaying lengths of water hose became viperous reptiles. You shuddered in fright when you walked on them or they brushed your careless hands. You imagined demons crouched on the tops of the buses, waiting to pounce on you. Your loneliness wore you down until you were unable to eat when lunch hour came, unable to read to pass the time when work was done.

When you were able to conquer the otherworld nightmares of the garage, your own life came forward to torment and blame. You remembered you never had any friends, you never succeeded, you were never loved. Haunting thoughts and impressions. Despairing fears and losses. All your failures came forward like a dark, tuneless choir. You realized what you were. A victim. I knew it happened. Sometimes, you tried to tell me about it.

For awhile, the night shift was your greatest battle, your finest hour. You reached out, panting and gasping, for the seniority that would free you. But I knew you couldn't win.

One night, I found you broken down. You were trying not to cry, but your hands trembled. You wanted to tell me about the nightmares in the garage, but I had already done the night shift before. I wouldn't listen to you because I felt pity and I would have changed shifts with you. Coldly, I turned away in anger, leaving you to your despair.

We weren't friends anymore, not that we had ever been. I had given you the night shift. I had seniority.

We found you one morning at five, when we came in to begin the morning shifts. You were dangling from one of the garage rafters near the front of the building, by the timeclock. You hung like some effigy at a high school football game, from three braided extension cords. A victim.

You were still like the sleeping monuments all around you. The blower came on and your corpse trembled. The boiler roared, as if in laughter, drowning out my cry of surprise and despair.

"My God," someone said. "He's hung himself."

There was a flurry of useless conversation and activity, an argument as to whether or not you should be left there until the police arrived. Someone phoned them, I suppose, because, moments later, they arrived with an ambulance.

I watched you dangling there while everyone turned away in some kind of mystical shame. I looked at you as if you were something surprising. I was oblivious to the confusion that buzzed around you. I couldn't think. I felt as mechanical as the buses. Finally, maddened by my anger, I turned away for fear I would senselessly punch at your carcass. Outside the garage, I puked all over the snowy sidewalk.

We found out later that you had punched out before hanging yourself. It seemed a curious circumstance to us that you had chosen to die on your own instead of company time. Somehow, you had finished all of your work, enduring every nightmare that was expected of you which you could have avoided. When you were braiding together the electric cords, you could have been home. You could have been sleeping comfortably in your bed, when you were gasping your life out beneath the rafters. The last act had been, in an ironic way, a victory. You had finished out the shift.

God, I hate you sometimes, Eric. I hate you because you managed to make me a victim, because I lost my seniority and because I'm not the way I was before you died.

They don't have a night shift now. No one would work it anyway. They'd all quit.

I'd quit too. Because of you, I don't have the strength I thought I did.

Barry Grills

A LONG LABOR

About six months after my short story A LONG LABOR *appeared in* Grain *in 1977, I heard from the magazine's editor, Caroline Heath. She wrote me a short note to say there had been a great deal of reaction to my story. She added—and a writer doesn't forget an observation like this—that many people found it disgusting. She further said that she still liked the story's honesty and seemed not to regret accepting it for publication for that reason, despite the negative reaction in some quarters, the details of which she never shared with me.*

A Long Labor is the first published appearance of a main protagonist who appeared in three other stories that appeared in both Quarry *and* Grain. *Phillip Barrett was also my first character to be presented in the second person. I had some success utilizing this point of view. I did not intend it to convey the imperative voice, as a few people suggested to me. No, I wanted readers to recognize themselves in a character who is neither always likeable nor morally upright. Characters like Phillip Barrett, despite their shortcomings, still have a great deal to say about what it is to be a human. I have never faltered from this view. While it is probably not politically correct— especially as this correctness is expressed in our current millennium—I believe much of what characters like Phillip Barrett have to say is said in honesty.*

A LONG LABOR

FRANTICALLY MARY GESTURES for your hand, then finding it, takes your fingers and brutally crushes them. It seems to help her alleviate her agony. You try to ignore her surprising strength because she is your wife about to have your first child.

What can you think about as the pains come and go? It is hard to formulate thoughts or ideas when she is gasping through contractions. Instead, you are aware only of your fatigue, a tiredness that makes you stare like an idiot at her transparent face etched with burning agony. Mary's exhaustion is physical. Yours, however, is spiritual. Her agony has a natural cause, but yours could represent some terrible mutation.

She curses again.

You smile like a man with only a dozen smiles left.

Knowing she does not curse the child that batters on the doorway into life, you realize she condemns the pain instead and, in the future, she will deny having cursed at all.

The agony recedes again and she collapses into the

pillow, smiling weakly. You wink at her and shrug, then quickly look away, afraid she will describe awful secrets and make you pain's accomplice.

"Relax," you mutter. "The nurse said you have to relax."

Mary scowls. When you are being your most helpful, it creates resentment.

"Are you okay?" There is more kindness in your voice and you are gesturing in futile compassion.

"No," she replies, smiling to make it a joke.

Conversation dies too easily. She releases your hand and closes her eyes. Suddenly you feel safe, even when you cannot remember what threatened you.

She is pale and clammy, and the race she has been running for hours has left her breathless. Her features, harsh at the best of times, seem chipped from granite. Yet, your Mary will be an attractive woman as long as she lives. She is as colorless as a black and white photo, her dark hair warped and torn into black, oily curls, but you can still see the woman you once loved.

You would like to say something you have not said before, but after five hours of labor room ordeal, your mind and mouth are empty. It does not matter though. Now that all instructions have been given efficiently and methodically, you prefer the silence. In silence you seem a considerate man. Deep inside, some lies become the truth.

Where are your emotions? Should they not be building gradually toward the ecstatic climax of the baby's birth? Your thoughts are very black. Now that labor has begun, you are very different from what you expected you would be. There is no optimism or hope, no concern or fear, no pride or anticipation. Even your sympathy for Mary's ordeal is half-hearted.

In place of all the responses you think normal, you feel tired and restless. You have failed to fool yourself. You can no longer pretend you were ready to be a father. An awkward truth, it is as hard to face as you are.

The contractions are not very close together yet. You have been told the first child can be difficult. You wish, for Mary's sake, it was all over. Now and then, when you can remember to concentrate, you time the gaps between her torrential pain. Why is it so difficult to think about something other than yourself?

"I hate this room," you say, glancing around to make sure it hasn't suddenly improved. "It's too green, too efficient and clean."

Mary looks at the ceiling. "I'm glad it's efficient. It makes me feel safe."

You shake your head. The room, in boasting about the successful births it has witnessed, is wickedly cynical. It seems to be laughing, as if it has some secret knowledge you will never learn.

"I thought birth was some kind of miracle," you mutter disparagingly. "But this room makes it look like nothing. If it happens every day or every hour, how can birth be a miracle?"

Mary pats your hand. "Of course it's a miracle, Phillip."

"I'm not so sure," you murmur. "I'd like to believe birth and death are miracles not some pointless exercise."

"Stop talking like that!"

You are quiet, silently ensnared by a vague anger in the pit of your stomach that makes your hands tremble and fills your mouth with spittle. The room is a foreign land, your wife some suffering stranger you happened upon. Those disquieting conclusions and the ghostly promise of your child, a usurper, make you want to say angry things.

You want to remind your pain-caressed wife, for instance, that your baby has originated in a swamp of sweat, saliva and sexual juices. Then, perhaps, the pale fulfilment that shares space on her face with agony will no longer stand between you. You want to say something that will make your wife forget she has purpose. The child inside her with its battering ram body gives her, as far as she is concerned, immortality. You, however, are going to die a purposeless life.

She takes your hand and shares a new contraction with you, then, when it subsides, frees you again, setting you adrift in your futility.

In your entire life, you have acknowledged nothing more than what you feel. Making love is something you can understand, but giving birth is not. God, your guilt makes you feel lonely. Mary can know things without feeling them inside but, if you do not feel something, you do not know it is there.

The din in the hall from which all labor rooms are entered grows in volume. You look at your watch.

"The nurses are changing shift."

Mary only smiles like some benevolent, patient monarch. Her slight reaction makes your words seem more inane than they really were. What you wouldn't do to avoid feeling barren.

"Hello, Mary," a voice says, moving in the doorway. "Hello, Phillip. How's our mother to be?"

Mary makes some gesture with her hand. "As well as can be expected," she responds.

Eleanor Bird stands still a moment, her hands on her hips. "Gosh, I don't know which one of you looks worse."

You laugh, a lovely feeling.

"I thought we might see you before I got out," Mary says. "I couldn't remember for sure whether you worked in maternity or not."

"For some time now," Eleanor replies, touching you as she passes toward your wife.

Eleanor Bird is an exciting woman. Seeing her again, you can remember occasions when there were other touches and flirtatious glances. Once, several months ago, you might have made love together. Opportunity, however, evaded you and your enthusiasm dissolved like sugar in passing circumstance.

She takes Mary's blood pressure and you hear exclusive conversation pass between them. It is not meant for your ears, so you do not listen. Instead, you examine Eleanor's marvelous legs and a wheaty sheaf of hair that touches her neck.

She turns and catches you looking. For an instant, you examine words in her eyes, then flick your gaze away

46

to her tentatively inviting smile. The momentary discovery would continue, but Mary renews her rendezvous with pain, gasping and cursing, waving frantically for your hand. This time, Eleanor is there, giving comfort to wife, then husband, then wife again like some perfect, bisexual wizard.

"Why don't you get yourself a coffee?" Eleanor says, turning and looking practical.

You shrug, not because it is a good idea, but because you wish she would look at you the way she did before.

"Okay," you mutter an eternity later.

"I'll take care of things here for now," Eleanor says, not bothering to look up.

IN THE FATHER'S WAITING ROOM, you are unreasonably enraged. You feel like a child who has received a gift, then had to return it. At the same time, you are stimulated by mental allusions; you have decided men are Prometheus. His insides are your sexuality, plucked, growing, then plucked again, day after day, forever. Except for making babies, you decide with exciting bitterness, women need nothing more than a sexual device—a vibrator, perhaps.

The waiting room is an enigma of proposed comfort and concerted dissatisfaction. The seating is comfortable and useful items such as as ashtrays, coffee dispensers and soft drink machines are at hand. Out in the hall, however, there are things that depress, that remind you of formidable disasters.

"Nurse? Bring me a glass of water?" Croaking and shrieking in agony, the sound of archaic womanhood.

"Can I have a cigarette?" It is a man this time, his voice wailing like an abandoned child's. "Please? I need to have a smoke."

An eternity later, a nurse replies: "Go to sleep, Mr. Adams."

He grows threatening. "I'm going to be sick. Give me a cigarette or I'm going to be sick. I'll puke all over the bed."

"That's enough, Mr. Adams!"

For a couple of minutes the wailing and sobbing continues. Then it ends or you stop listening.

You think of things pathetically ironic, babies that come into the world wailing for food, rest and clean underwear, old people leaving the world the very same way.

"Christ," you complain aloud, falling exhausted along the couch. "What's going on in here?"

HOW LONG LATER IS IT that you come awake strangling in the phlegm in your throat? You have dreamed you were a salmon. You struggled upstream and spawned, then you began to drown in your uselessness.

As you open your eyes, you catch someone staring at you.

"How would you like to be a seahorse?" you murmur in his direction.

"I beg your pardon?" he replies in a nervous voice.

"If you were a seahorse," you say, "you would be upstairs right now and your wife would be down here."

"Oh?"

"It's true," you say quietly, with just the hint of

professorial smile. "Male seahorses are the ones who carry the offspring."

"I didn't know that," the man mumbles, stealing a brief, worried glance out the door.

"It's true," you say again, enjoying your delirium. "Of course that's better than being a spider. I mean, how would you like to be married to a black widow spider?"

The man does not respond. Instead, he mops his sweaty brow with a tri-colored handkerchief and loosens the knot in his tie.

"You know why they're called black widow spiders?"

Waiting for a reply is spoiling the fun. You plunge ahead.

"I'll tell you why. Because, after mating, the black widow spider eats her husband. How do you like that?"

"I didn't know."

You nod smugly like a philosopher-king.

"Is this the first one for you?" you ask later.

"Yes," he says in relief. "How about you?"

"Oh I'm not having a baby," you say. "I'm just doing a little research. I'm studying the mating habits of the human male."

The man is no fool. He knows when to remain silent. He mops his brow again and readjusts himself so he doesn't rumple his suit. Then he runs a hand over his oily, dark hair.

"How often do you mate?" you ask.

YOU HAVE BEEN TRYING TO TIME the millennium between each contraction. It seems an impossible task now that hours have gone by and your confusion has multiplied.

"Eleanor says he'll be a big one," Mary tells you. "Eight pounds anyway."

"Really?"

"Sure. That's why I'm having so much trouble."

"Everything's all right, isn't it?"

"Of course it is."

There is nothing else to say. You think about your obligations and how they will increase when the baby is born. You do not mind responsibility if it stands alone, but when it displaces enjoyment or pleasure, you resist it and feel ensnared. You keep looking at the green sterility of the room, knowing Mary is achieving some kind of glorious satisfaction here while you would like to be somewhere else, achieving something of your own. Maybe in Africa on the veldt in a jeep, learning the ropes from a great white hunter.

You dare not say anything to Mary. Although she is often the source of many of your resentments, you do not want to hurt her. It is easier to lie or pretend.

When Eleanor comes in again, she touches your shoulder with her long fingers. Suddenly the mud in your brain is filtered away; everything is very clear. Her touch has created a feeling you can understand. There is no confusion in the sensations she creates. Confusion comes only when you try to know what you should feel or would feel or could feel.

"Get another coffee, Phillip," Eleanor says. "I'll come

down in a minute and we'll have a little chat."

You peer into her eyes and nod, then head for the door.

Going out, you glance at Mary to see if she has noticed anything, but she has entered the glory of her agony. She hears nothing but the coming child.

"MY HUSBAND WANTED TO START A FAMILY," Eleanor says near closed eyelids in the corner of the waiting room. "I guess I wasn't ready."

She opens her eyes and you know she is waiting for a reaction.

"How did you resolve it?" you ask.

She is quite amused. "I thought you knew. Gerry and I separated. It was never resolved at all."

"That's too bad," you reply, feeling excited, then foolish because you care.

"I guess so," she murmurs.

She leans her head back on the top of the couch and closes her eyes again.

You watch her closely, tapping the top of your empty coffee cup with restless fingers. Inside you, there is an insatiable urge to touch her, perhaps on the cheek or the neck. She is so pale and pretty, so long, her legs resting on the coffee table beside an old issue of Time Magazine.

She wants you to be lecherous. Of that you can be sure. At the same time, something inside you is tremendously emotional and you know you are chasing dreams again. You want Eleanor to be the woman you have promised yourself since your youth, the one whose embrace will eliminate the loneliness in your vision of things. Perhaps she can be the passion you feel and the passion you want to receive.

No. Long ago, you have given up on the woman who dances exotically in your ideals. You remind yourself it is better to be lecherous and reach at least half of the perfect woman.

"I don't know if I'll be a good father," you say, preferring talk to your bitter and possibly erroneous conclusions.

"You should have thought about that nine months ago," Eleanor replies disdainfully.

"It wasn't up to me." You stand and find the window. "I didn't know we were conceiving. I thought we were making love."

When you turn, Eleanor is smiling something obscene and clairvoyant.

"You're a strange one," she mutters finally, passing sentence.

You are white with anger because you still want to touch her. Her love, after all, though free of the urge to reproduce, will only half include you.

Standing at the window, a fleet of female bodies known by you before your marriage, and since, pass like freight trains in your memory. Naked breasts and thrashing thighs, glistening tears and sad, optimistic whimpers. The seeds of your impotence have been planted long ago and you can feel them growing like jungle foliage.

"I wouldn't hate women so much, if I didn't love them," you chant like a curse. You hope your words are fiercely mysterious so that, in a woman's eyes, you become more attractive.

Eleanor has come up behind you, her reflection in the glass before your face. You feel her hand touch the pockets of perspiration on your back. At first it dances lightly, then it strokes and caresses. Her fingers sting your flesh for a few seconds more, then they are gone.

You do not want to turn around or reach for her, but you cannot help yourself. When you do, she crosses the room and disappears through the doorway. Your outstretched arms are foolishly optimistic, sadly empty.

Sleep comes quickly when you lie down on the couch. You dream you are the monster at the bottom of the loch.

IT IS DARK OUTSIDE THE HOSPITAL when your son is born. Mary is radiant, but you are a star that has burned itself out. She tells you about the birth, how the baby came into the world emptying his bowels on the doctor who went to fetch him.

"Isn't he wonderful?" Mary says, cradling and kissing the newborn stranger.

"Except for the pain," you mutter, feeling sorry and somehow to blame.

"All forgotten. I can't even remember it."

You nod and look at your wrinkled, tiny child. Somewhere you find the courage to smile. What should you feel? What will happen now? You have no idea what you will do with a son and what he will do with you.

Outside, you take several deep breaths of the voluptuous night air. You check your watch. It is just after midnight. As you walk between the cars, headlights shine on your back and on the pavement in front of you. You move to the left side of the lot, but the car stops as if you are still in the way. When you turn to look, it pulls up beside you.

"Need a lift?" Eleanor says through the open window.

"I have my own car."

You watch one another for a moment or two.

"You're welcome to come along with me," she says finally.

The night is filled with stars, splattered with glittering promises. You cross behind the car, then reach for the door handle. You climb inside to try to find your passion.

A GAME WITH ADONIS

A GAME WITH ADONIS, *another short story about main protagonist Phillip Barrett, was published three times by the end of the 1970s. It appeared in the winter 1977 issue of* Quarry Magazine *and then subsequently in* '78 Best Canadian Stories *as well as in an anthology edited by George Bowering, entitled* Great Canadian Sports Stories. *Both anthologies were published by* Oberon Press.

By the time of its first publication, Gail Fox had taken over as editor of Quarry *and this first issue of her editorship was billed as a Kingston issue; I lived in Belleville still, but close enough. Not long afterwards, I would begin chasing some newspaper jobs, going first to Kapuskasing, ON, then to Barrie, ON. I was on the move once again in Barrie—packing furiously in a farmhouse I shared with various television news personnel—to take a job at* The Reporter *in Gananoque, ON, when the telephone rang. It was Myrna Metcalf, wife of John*

Metcalf, and she asked if I would give permission for A Game With Adonis *to be included in the '78 Best Canadian Stories anthology. You bet I would. John Metcalf and Clark Blaise were the editors. I was thrilled. Ultimately, I kept company in this book with Alice Munro, Hugh Hood, Joyce Carol Oates, Kent Thompson and Elizabeth Spencer, to name only some.*

I'm not sure how long I'd been in Gananoque when I heard from John Metcalf again. He reached me at the newspaper and told me George Bowering wanted A Game With Adonis *for an anthology he was putting together. Coordinates were exchanged and I received a contract for this next publication. If my Grade Nine teacher Miss Phillips could see me now—there I was in a short story collection with Clark Blaise, Hugh Hood, Hugh Garner, Mordecai Richler, Andreas Schroeder, Kenneth Smale, Dave Godfrey, David Helwig, Matt Cohen, Hanford Woods and Morley Callaghan. In fact, I had studied Morley Callaghan's* A Cap For Steve *in high school.*

Shortly afterward I met John Metcalf and Hugh Hood in Kingston. They were signing and selling their books—I believe it was at The Printed Passage book store. In my copy of John's General Ludd, *which I purchased that day, John wrote, "For Barry, fellow sufferer." This autograph is one of my prized possessions for the acknowledgment it contained. By this time, I was finding being a writer a lonely and under-appreciated occupation.*

Even my parents were unwittingly adding to the isolation. Upon a visit to their home when they lived just west of Toronto, I noticed a copy of '78 Best Canadian Stories on the shelf of their bookcase. It lurked there among a wide array of historical fiction and romance novels my mother enjoyed. I commented on how difficult it must have been to find in the town where they lived.

"We had to order it," my mother admitted.

"So what did you think of my story?" I asked.

I don't know which parent, father or mother—they were both present—admitted neither of them had read it.

"How come?" I wanted to know.

"We knew it'd be weird," my mother said.

That cock-eyed voice thing, I guess.

Yet a Books In Canada review of the Bowering anthology focused at least some of its attention on my story, describing the second person viewpoint as "so successful, the reader squirms in self-recognition."

I'll take it.

A GAME WITH ADONIS

YOU LOOK AT YOUR MISTRESS, Melody James, and your eyes touch. Like an impassioned embrace or a long, slow caress, her glance excites and torments. Your expression shows warmth because you are a little in love with her. Her eyes are flirtatious because she is promiscuous and loves no-one. Sometimes you think she enjoys the danger of someone almost catching her.

Her eyes are large and provocative, a daring blue. You feel empty when she flicks them away, capturing your wife, Mary, and your son, Danny, in her vision. A smile widens on her lips and she comes over to affectionately touch Mary's arm. Briefly, she picks up your two-year-old son and kisses his cheek. When he squirms, she puts him down, babbling some woman-friendship nonsense that makes your Mary laugh.

Mary has told you that Melody is her best friend. Sometimes, despite the intimate nature of your treachery, you actually believe it.

There are more greetings. The other women, all wives of your friends, are scattered about on blankets in colorful array. Reacquaintance among you is offhand and casual.

The acknowledged friendship of the nine couples in your group exists on two levels. Together, you share many characteristics—financial worth, status, age and interests. Although special friendships have formed between two or three couples, the perimeter of the larger group sustains your basic companionship.

Now and then a few minor alliances are formed and at times, tiny conflicts develop. Sometimes a harmless gossip circulates the neighborhood. Yet, because you and your friends socialize so regularly, such talk is almost pointless. Already, everyone is familiar with almost everything about the group's members.

In the past, you have likened your friends to rooms in a house. What good would it do if the living-room gossiped to a bedroom about the bathroom? You realize that none of them will do anything to weaken the structure of their fraternity. In that light, you are amazed that no-one knows about you and Melody.

You watch the children for a moment. Your son is the youngest in the group, but the oldest is only five, the others in between. You and your friends share so many social engagements and have such a good time doing it, the children are almost brothers and sisters together.

Feeling secure and content, you study the group, mentally counting heads. Except for Mark and Nancy Spencer, you have all arrived. Camp has been pitched. Each blanket tilts down the hill toward the football field. A collection of unopened picnic baskets is scattered about, but the food will not be eaten until after the game.

The women talk in crests and troughs, waiting. Except when Melody speaks, when you listen lovingly to the musical lilt of her voice, you are oblivious to their conversation. Instead, you think about football and the importance of playing well.

You find all the women attractive. Often, when you study your friends, you feel you wear a badge of accomplishment at being included. Many times, Mary has said you have an inherent inferiority complex and that is why you feel humble. She has also said that you exaggerate the group's beauty, but you know you care more than she does. Mary has always been distant in her friendships, when you have cared too much. Yet, knowing your weakness, you cannot help feeling a tremendous contentment with your friends because they are attractive and materially similar to you.

You glance at Melody again. There is something

stimulating about the agony of not being able to touch her. You imagine putting your fingertips on her cheek or running your palm down the sleek length of her blond hair. You would remember more, perhaps, if she did not glance up at you and hold you with her eyes, appeasing you for the moment, before safely looking away again.

There is a tremendous disparity between what Melody appears to be and what she really is. Small and delicate, it is unimaginable that she can make love in the impassioned, almost violent way she does. Her slim fragility implies an innocence she does not possess. Her lovemaking is surprisingly uninhibited, but her cruelty and her ability to torment are startling. At times, when you are making love, you suspect that she is laughing at you, a vicious laughter that seems to gleam in her eyes.

When you desperately want her to understand your feelings, she is cold and unreceptive. Yet, when you try, in some small way, to deceive her, she cannot be fooled. She toys with your passion as if it were an elegant but mundane meal, until finally it builds and recedes at her command. She has transformed your love for her into something as foolish as childhood adoration. Frantically, you wish she loved you. Then everything would be all right.

Suddenly despairing, you turn away from her. You look at Mary instead. She is not cruel and she does not torment. You are very fond of her, but your passion for her has disappeared somewhere. You don't know when or how.

Mary is very strong and stubborn. She always knows

where she is going, what she is doing and why she is doing it. She is an excellent wife and mother, and she loves you. It is not her fault that you must experience the same kind of love you feel inside. Sometimes an idyllic poem. Often a torrent of emotion. Watching her, you feel a vague guilt. You wish you loved her or, at least, were content not to.

You study the men on the field. Restless to begin, they toss the football back and forth. The impending game has taken on a seriousness no-one intended when the idea was first conceived. Although you have decided to play flag football, the game will be rough. A good-natured rivalry exists between you and all of you possess a fierce pride.

Mary asks you to help her spread the blanket. You comply immediately because she has never tolerated delay.

"It's a perfect day for football," she says with a smile.

You nod, wanting to be dismissed.

But Danny runs up from somewhere, encircling your legs with his arms. You reach down and tousle his hair, but you do not pick him up. Satisfied, he runs back to the others.

Inside, you suffer an obscure uneasiness. Is it a premonition or some kind of guilt? To avoid thinking about it, you cast one more loving glance at Melody, but she and Mary are talking, touching one another in laughing friendship.

"I'm going down to warm up," you say.

Mary looks up and waves you off with her hand.

"Well go ahead," she says.

You trot down the hill to the field. Your muscles are tight and ancient.

The sun is brilliant and exceptionally warm for late September. Although only an hour before the temperatures were crisp, the men are sweating and have stripped down to their T-shirts.

"Hello, boys," you yell from the sidelines.

Someone throws you a pass.

ON THE FIELD, YOUR MOVEMENTS are awkward and uncomfortable. Just when you want to perform well for Melody, you suspect you will fail. Apprehensively, you wait for the Spencers to arrive so the game can begin. You keep telling yourself to calm down, but Melody's image in your mind or a glance in her direction from the field nourishes your fears and sustains your haunting doubts.

You try not to look to the sidelines, but you do and you see that the women have moved down the hill to cheer you on. Suddenly, you feel naked and lonely.

Melody has the cure in her eyes. If she looks at you with even a microbe of love, you will be empowered to tremendous physical heights. But you know better than that. She will wait until that nebulous moment, when she feels you have earned her glance, before you will know the excitement of her eyes. Melody will build your anticipation first. She will bring you to your knees. She knows you are in love with her.

Your affair began a month ago. To you, it was an

accident. You wanted it, but you thought it was impossible because, this time, you were in love. When it began, you couldn't believe your good fortune.

You told her that first night, that your passion for her was new, from a source you could not understand. You said you couldn't help yourself, but she saw through your pretentious innocence.

"I know about you, Phillip," she said. "Why are you lying to me?"

"I'm not lying," you protested, somehow ashamed.

Although she did not argue further, her smile continued to insinuate her point of view. And she derived great enjoyment telling you how she had connived the affair's beginning.

She was a flame of passion when you made love. Yet, at the same time, she was a cold extinguisher on the blaze of your emotions. That was why you could never share her candour. You were in love and you had too much to lose, even belief in your own feelings.

You realized that if you ever left her, you could be readily replaced. The pain caused by this knowledge was as potent as your ardour. Already, she had you in her grasp.

She wanted to know about your other affairs. She listened to your responses, but when you tried to explain some of the sadnesses in your heart or the kind of ecstasy you sought, she looked away, suddenly disinterested. Even the woman you loved could not share your unique perception.

Now, a month later, you do not understand

anything. You only know what you feel—love and frustration, two separate emotional links somehow chained together.

You drop the football when it is thrown to you and, as you bend to pick it up, you look at Melody. She laughs with the other women, ignoring you.

Ironically, however, your Mary is watching. You smile at her and feel guilt. You remember that love is an awkward thing because you understand its sensation but not its direction. As a feeling, you believe love is almost perfect. Yet, between two people, you have seen it hopeless and unfair, imbalanced and cruel. Mary loves you, but you do not love her. You love Melody, but she does not love you. It is too bad you and Mary do not love each other.

Suddenly angry, you hurl the football at one of your companions. It spins crazily, in mocking, spiraling laughter.

FINALLY, THE SPENCERS ARRIVE. Suddenly, a strange ambivalence infiltrates the group. You sense it at once. A stranger in your midst is causing the almost perceptible uproar among your friends. You have expected him because he is Mark's brother brought along to even up the sides, but you have never met him before and you did not imagine what he would be like.

He is as handsome as a god. All of you, men and women alike, are startled by his provocative appearance. You feel an animal envy.

His name is Stephen. He is at least six feet tall, lean

like a wood carving, chipped with muscle. He slouches self-consciously because he faces many strangers, yet he possesses a casual confidence and innate agility that advertises an extraordinary athletic ability.

You have heard women say they find lean men more sexually attractive than stocky men. You know instantly that Stephen Spencer is exactly what they mean. He has all the physical qualities you have heard women describe as attractive. Large blue eyes with long, lazy lashes. A mass of dark, curly hair that manages to be orderly even in disarray. While, reluctant teeth.

Herb James, Melody's husband, nudges you. "Feel outclassed?"

You manage a smile. "Who wouldn't?"

"Mark says he's a hell of a football player," Herb mutters. "Plays in college. Does the hundred in ten flat. A real golden boy, our Stephen. Great marks in class and a whiz on the football field. I'll bet he has no trouble in the girls' dormitory either."

"I suppose not," you reply.

Mark looks like his brother's agent. You notice the difference because you know him very well. He exhibits a smug self-assurance and pride you have never seen before. You know he has seen similar reactions before from people encountering his brother for the first time and, in a way you find strictly perverse, he is enjoying himself.

"Bastard," you mumble under your breath.

You watch Mark introduce him to the women on the

sidelines. You study Melody very carefully, searching for some indication of her reaction to the young man who has innocently but forcefully crashed your party.

You do not look for flirtatiousness because you have seen it many times before. You have hardened yourself to it because it is an inevitable part of Melody's character. Instead, fearfully, you await some display of her greedy lust.

But your judgment is impaired. You cannot be certain of what you see or do not see. Do their eyes really meet the way you think they do? Do her fingertips really linger on the palm of his hand when they are introduced? Does she really turn to watch him move away from her to someone else? Is she thinking the things you imagine she does? You have no way of knowing. The most frustrating inadequacy of all.

Even the other women are acting strangely. Their embarrassment is conspicuous to you. They are flustered, you suspect, because they have not had the opportunity to prepare for this moment. Even Mary, who has the ability to ignore anything sensuous, is awkward. Usually insensitive to many emotions and hungers, she too displays a subtle excitement.

Mark brings the young man onto the field. You glance at Melody again and she briefly catches your eye. Is there mocking cruelty in her eyes or are you confounded by your envy and jealousy? You cannot be sure.

You look at Stephen and, although you know it is wrong, you feel an intense hatred. When your name is mentioned in introduction, you nod at him and turn away. Your knuckles, on the football, are white with strain.

THE FOOTBALL GAME IS A DISASTER. You dance among its incidents like a drunken phantom. Your lack of concentration seriously hampers your ability. Frequently, you find yourself looking toward the sidelines at Melody and, although you can only suspect, you sense her watching the young student. Your agony sticks in your stomach like an undigested meal.

Your team huddles. Heavy breathing. You try very hard to concentrate on the game.

"What's the score?" you ask stupidly.

"Jeezus, Phil," Herb says. "What's the matter with you? They have three touchdowns. We haven't put a damned point on the board."

You nod. Herb and the others look at you as if you have a mental illness.

"Sorry," you say. "I can't think."

"Yeah," Herb replies, not the least pacified by your flimsy excuse.

"Listen, boys," someone in the huddle says. "We have to stop that Spencer kid. He's all over the god-damn field. And two of those touchdowns are his."

"I know," someone else says. "But I can't even catch the bastard, let alone pull the flags out of his belt."

"Okay," Herb says impatiently. "Let's try to flood him with receivers. We'll all run right at him. In the confusion, we should be able to complete a pass."

Everyone nods in agreement. You come out of the huddle.

Time passes. You lose the ball to Mark's team and they score another touchdown. Suddenly, you and Herb stand on your twenty yard-line, awaiting the kickoff.

"We have to stop that guy," Herb says. "We have to do something soon."

"I know," you reply. "I know."

"We look like a bunch of jerks."

You turn to the sidelines again. All eyes seem to be on the winners. Inevitably, you capture Melody in your gaze, but she pays no attention. Impressions leap and tumble in your imagination, shadowy figures that grow clearer behind your eyes. You see your impassioned Melody naked and glistening with sweat. You see the vacant ghost of her ecstasy etched upon her face. Finally, worst of all, you imagine the lean, muscular frame of Stephen Spencer all over her like a hurricane of passion. You hear and see and hate. You . . .

"Jeezus Christ," Herb yells.

You snap out of it. To your left the ball bounces on the turf, then skitters crazily away toward your goal line.

"Pick it up, for Chrissake," Herb yells.

You lurch toward the ball, the sound of pounding feet all around you. You do not realize you are off balance until it is too late. Suddenly, you fall on your chest on the ground. There is a brief spasm of pain, but it is buried under the colourful splendour of your shame.

You look up. Stephen Spencer has bent, on the run, over the ball. He picks it up in his competent, graceful fingers. Yet, two of your teammates are on him, each grasping frantically at his squirming body and the tantalizing motion of the flags on each side of his belt. He struggles toward the goal line, twisting and turning. In a few seconds, your teammates will lose their hold. Melody will see him score again.

You jump to your feet. Something exciting and rich surges through your body. Like locomotive pistons, your feet move without control. You have focused on the young man's undulating hips and, in a second, you are rushing at full speed in that direction. Your brain is dull of reason, sharp with emotion. The collision is only an instant away, but you accelerate. Then, just as his body is about to break away from your teammates, you throw yourself against him. There is a grunt of surprise as he loses balance and you both fall to the ground. Even then you do not give up and your legs are pounding, doubling your force as you slam into his fallen, twisted carcass.

"Oh God!"

The snap of his shattering leg echoes across the field, followed by a shrill scream of pain. The football spurts loose like a laughing leprechaun, bounces a couple of times, then becomes motionless.

Suddenly, it is all over. Everything is too late. There is a tremendous commotion as the men run up to clutch futilely at Stephen Spencer's writhing body. You are on your feet, gesturing here and there as if you can do something useful, knowing you cannot.

"I'm sorry," you say. "I'm so sorry."

You actually mean it, but the more you say it the less

believable it becomes. No-one looks at you. They are afraid.

The women run across the field. As you absently watch them coming, something hits you in the back and you stagger. When you turn, you see the red-faced outrage of Mark Spencer.

"You bastard," he yells. "You dirty bastard."

The other men take hold of his arms. He squirms to be free, but they pull him away, talking to him.

"C'mon, Mark. It was an accident. Just a stupid accident."

"I'm sorry," you say again.

No-one listens.

Herb talks to Mark now. "C'mon," he says. "We all saw it. It's just the way he fell. Phil wasn't trying to hurt him. It's just a bit of bad luck. One of those things."

"That's right," you say. "I couldn't help it. I was off balance."

Mark begins to calm down. He breaks free of the other men and bends over his brother.

"Has someone called a god-damn ambulance?" he yells.

Two men immediately run across the field.

No-one will look at you. The men don't know if you have done what you did on purpose. They don't know if they are capable of the same thing. The women have decided you are a cruel monster whether the injury was an accident or not. That and what you know you have done, hurts you most.

"I'm sorry," you murmur again. The last time.

Some of the men pick up the injured youth and begin to carry him off the field. Every so often, he shrieks in pain. Most of the women follow along behind, like mourners behind a coffin. Mary touches your arm and Herb puts his hand on your shoulder in weak reassurance. No-one speaks.

You sense someone watching you. You look up. You see the glint of laughter in Melody's eyes.

Barry Grills

MARATHON

MARATHON *did not appear until December, 1987. Again, it was published in* Quarry. *Again, the main protagonist was Phillip Barrett. Again, as in all Phillip Barrett stories, the viewpoint was expressed in the second person. This story, as I remember it, was the one grudgingly accepted with the "cock-eyed voice" remark.*

It was during this period that I detected a certain conservatism entering the world of the short story generally and the placing of short stories in literary magazines specifically. While the real reason the short story and I were losing interest in one another surrounded my growing preference for the novel, I was also aware that my stories were getting more difficult to place. Experimental in style, politically prickly in most cases, they were often difficult to place and Canada's literary magazines were not accepting them.

The other development in the short story market was

that the pay cheques for these stories had declined immensely. My first short story, Talent, had netted me one hundred dollars. My third to last story to be published in a literary magazine, sixteen years later, earned me fifteen dollars and a note of apology for the amount from Alistair MacLeod. Grants were shrinking. I anticipated, in the not-too-distant future, literary magazines would expect writers to write for publication for free. What I did not anticipate, though, was that so many younger writers would not only accept this development but, strangely, embrace it. The relationship that had developed between me and the world of magazines at the end of the 1960s and early 1970s was already coming to an end as I published new stories at the end of the 1980s.

I view Marathon as my first published story in a new era of short fiction for writers and literary magazines. These times would ultimately evolve to the point where the short story and I couldn't retain our interest in one another.

MARATHON

THERE ARE THINGS YOU POSSESS, others that belong to Jason; that is how it is between you. For this reason, you let Jason go on alone when he bursts away from you on the final lap of a five-mile practice run around your high school track. You let him pull away because his colourful finish was secretly expected by you both.

Jason will win the race scheduled for Saturday morning. The newspapers have said so and he knows it is true. Last year's winner, he has no real competition and his victory is taken for granted. But for you, his friend, there is something else. The race *belongs* to Jason. It is *his*.

As you run now through the May sunshine, he moves further ahead of you, the treads in his sneakers tossing back dirt too irrelevant to be considered an insult. You drift back and let him go, feeling admiration. Although you are surprisingly untired yourself, you are too fascinated by his final burst of speed to even try to keep up. Jason running and winning. You share in his skill the way you share the ugly rasp of your breathing and the pain in your belly and legs. And maybe, just for a second, your pride in Jason is ever so slightly tarnished by your envy.

You catch up to him finally and the two of you walk around the track together, regaining your breaths, returning your bodies to normal.

"How did it feel?" you ask.

"Great." And his gaze down the track is intense. "I had some left over. I can feel it."

"Good. You'll take it again, Jas. Just like last year."

He nods, then thinks to be humble. "I hope so."

"No problem."

Jason sweats. The perspiration forms in silver beads on his forehead and they cling like doomed mountain climbers to the ends of his rich, dark curls. He looks fierce and proud, nearly Neanderthal, carved from stone, as beautiful as ancient Greece.

"I hope the weather's this good Saturday," he says as you stroll around the track. "It's warm today. It loosens you up."

"Yeah."

There is a sidelong glance, as if only now, you have begun to exist. "What about you, Phil? A good run?"

You give the afterthought question an afterthought answer. "Not bad."

Because Jason is going to win the race Saturday, how you run it won't matter. His asking, in the grand scheme of things, is only politeness. You are friends. At the borders of your respective kingdoms, you exchange diplomacies.

Near the bleachers on the edge of the track, you see Donna Lewis waiting alone, separate from the activities of departure around the high school exits and parking lots. She stands there against the sun, in silhouette, Jason's girl, waiting for him to come back to her. They are the school's most melodic duet, each as handsome as the other, but sometimes in your most secret thoughts, you vandalize their perfect portrait with tiny slashings of lust. Sometimes you imagine running your fingers through her cornsilk hair or along her naked body. Sometimes, when you encounter her, some powerful discomfort gnaws at your stomach and you feel a frustration that is nearly anger.

Her eyes will be blue.

"There's Donna," you say, trying to mask your guilt.

But when Jason does not reply, you know he remains preoccupied with the race on Saturday, His various challenges, though they come and go, are profound infatuations. They die quickly in spite of the intensity of their brief life in his heart.

When you reach Donna at the bleachers, she kisses Jason hastily, then hands him his t-shirt. While you watch, he quickly shrugs into the shirt and runs his fingers through his hair, rearranging it. Donna doesn't ask him about the run. Although Jason is a champion who wins things for her, she seems detached from his greatness and even from her own. Their aloofness is almost royal, their caring for one another an affair of state. Even coveting Donna at times, you know you would want more warmth from her than she seems to give to Jason. You would want her to be in love with you.

On occasion, you and Jason have discussed love, but he finds the subject embarrassing. You have even wondered if love comes too easily to him, that he denies its existence because it has never had to be won. Perhaps love is a not a race he wants to run.

But Jason is making arrangements. "We're going to shower," he tells Donna. "We'll meet you at the car."

"Okay," she says, taking his keys.

His car is not far away, gleaming in the sunlight, a gift in honour of his seventeenth birthday.

You watch her walk away and feel traces of someone's loneliness. Yours or Donna's or even Jason's.

IN THE SHOWERS, the steam rises and mingles with some mystifying glee that exists between you. Naked and intimate, you feel drawn closer together, but remain embarrassed and apart. There has been something electrical in the run, in sharing the twenty laps around the track, perhaps even about the way you share Donna each in his own way, but you are naked now and want to hide. Jason makes sport of your exposure. He chases you around the locker room, flicking his towel at your buttocks until they turn red and you howl in outrage. The game passes away, a bond that has wedged itself between careless explanations of your friendship.

"Do you think you'll marry Donna someday?" you ask Jason while you dress.

Startled by the question at first, he does not reply.

You feel caught and grow embarrassed.

"What kind of questions is that?" Jason's voice is almost angry. "Who thinks about marriage at our age?"

"I dunno. I do sometimes."

"Shit."

When you shrug, Jason comes to your rescue, as he has so often in the past. You suspect he derives satisfaction from saving you from your emotional self. When your feelings make you foolish, Jason calms you down. Your resentment at his superior attitude has been tempered by the gratitude you feel because he has shown you when to reel in your emotions and protect them from predators.

"Donna's not the kind of girl I see myself marrying," he says after a time, zipping up his fly and waiting for you to tie your sneakers.

"How come?"

"I guess it's because she's too good looking in the wrong way."

"Too sexy, you mean."

"You've noticed, I see." His grin is merciless, impudent.

"Sure I've noticed."

"Sexual designs on my girl," he says, giving you a shove and laughing.

"Just admiring your taste."

Your near-challenge goes ignored. Jason feels no threat. Donna belongs to him like the trophy at the end of the race on Saturday. You are his friend. To try to take her away would be an unnatural act. Yet, because you believe in love, some things become more and more impossible.

DONNA SLIDES OVER TO THE MIDDLE of the seat, letting you sit in the front with them. But you are temporarily ignored as she and Jason laugh together over the incidents of the day. Donna's leg touches yours because you sit so close to one another and your skin nearly aches. Does she do it on purpose? Wondering, you want to break the touch and move your leg away, an act of defiance, but you do not have the willpower. All the way home, you cling to your enmeshment in her heat.

THAT NIGHT, BECAUSE IT IS WEDNESDAY, Carol comes over so you can do your homework together. In the dining room, you sit across the table from one another and struggle through chemical formulae she understands a good deal better than you. Having done this so many times together, it is natural to be with her. Yet, this evening, you feel elongated by the remains of your excitement over Donna. The sensation obscures Carol and the bond you have enjoyed with her in the past.

Lately she has become a curiosity to you, but never more than tonight. Tonight she looks almost new because your being together is so aged. For many months now, Carol has been pretty and loyal, your friend. Tonight, however, your love for her falls short of the pinnacles of feeling of which you are capable. Your emotions are so keen they can split an arrow in a bullseye; tonight, it isn't enough to be able to simply hit the target.

You feel sad, nearly disappointed. As you work, you glance up from your books and guiltily admire her auburn hair. You toy with the idea that you should labour to make her wonderful again. But you fail, even when she catches you looking at her and interprets your fascination as caring. Although Carol can touch your heart, she no longer touches your sexuality. At night, before sleep, you have sometimes tried to transform her into someone you can physically desire, but the concept of an erotic Carol is difficult to sustain. She has no mystery anymore. She is too understood to be sexually enticing, an idea too uncomplicated. Somehow, because she claims to love you in return, Carol has lost some of her desirability. Although you do not want to fall in love only with women on pedestals the rest of your life, it makes you angry that there may be no other alternative.

After you finish your schoolwork, you go downstairs to watch television together. There, on the couch, you hold hands and chat through the commercials. But even when Carol laughs in the way you used to enjoy, or leans her head on your shoulder, you repress a brittle annoyance. Her actions achieve nothing more than an interference with the exquisite memory of the touch of Donna's leg, a touch that still aches its way through your bloodstream. Ashamed, you feel ugly and abscessed, some sore that will not heal.

THE DAY OF THE RACE is cold and countless runners huddle together in nervous little groups. There are a number of spectators from the participating schools, but the scene is somewhat anticlimactic. The newspaper has sent a photographer who takes time to snap some pictures of Jason doing deep knee bends before moving away to wait for the race to begin, visibly bored. Elsewhere there are school coaches and friends, parents and girlfriends of the running hopefuls.

Although virtually every competitor has run the course in practice, the streets, hills and valleys along the route are discussed in tense whispers as unexplored territory. The course is four and a half miles long and it ends here in the park where it will shortly begin.

Studying the activity around you, you feel the nagging nervousness that the others must share. The park is a hubbub of confused activity. Although some of the runners try to warm up against the unexpected cold of the day, most of them just mill around, wanting things to get started and finally end. Some of the competitors are more intense, glancing earnestly at the large silver trophy on a nearby table that will go to the victor. But the trophy is Jason's. Everyone seems to know that.

Jason stops exercising.

"How do you feel?" you ask him.

"Tight." Still, although he has complained, he appears unconcerned.

You stand there a moment, marveling at your friend. But this morning, your affection for him is marred by some new dislike. Covering up, you extend your hand. "Give it hell, Jas."

He shakes your hand, surprised. "Thanks, Phil. You too."

Carol has been chatting along the sidelines with friends, but suddenly she catches your eye and smiles. Last night she gave you a St. Christopher's medal for luck and now it dangles on a chain around your neck. You give her a grin then look away, standing there, not knowing what to do.

Jason has moved away to talk to Donna and you watch them for a time. There are clusters of school acquaintances around them, nearly worshipful. Jason smiles and answers their questions while Donna stands apart in cool detachment. You admire her beauty, her breasts in a thick, beige sweater, her hair so perfect in the breeze pervading the park.

Then, suddenly, she turns and catches you looking.

You feel she has seen the hunger on your face. Donna nearly smiles, using her eyes to flirt, until you look away, feeling foolish. Agitated, you find the medal on your chest, Carol's medal, and you toy with it. A second later, you notice Donna coming over.

"Ready for the big race?" she says.

"Yeah. I guess so."

"It's kind of cold."

"Yeah. Jason says he feels tight. But he'll win in the end anyway."

She stares at you, her expression inexplicable. "Everybody seems so sure about it."

"Something pretty strange would have to happen to change it."

She is thoughtful for a moment, then amazingly reaches up with a kiss. "For luck," she says, turning away and moving to the sidelines again.

When you glance at Jason, he simply grins. Donna belongs to him; the kiss was nothing. You feel a deep anger at his self-assurance. For the first time in your friendship, you wonder if he is arrogant. The thought is profoundly disquieting; because you share in his weakness, you resent him for pointing out your mutual imperfection.

Then the race officials begin calling the competitors to the starting line and you become entangled in the confusion of the race. The next few minutes are alien to you, as if they are happening to someone else. Although you have no stake in Jason's race, you are suddenly nervous, and several visions bustle through your mind like Christmas shoppers in a department store. Donna's kiss. Jason's grin. Carol. The crowds of racers and the report of the starting pistol. The nearly thunderous sound of running feet. The morning's chill and your vital, supercharged body, cold then warming up.

The race begins to stretch itself out, something historical, a map of nearly puzzling purpose that you want to ennoble you as a participant. You and your fellow runners keep passing one another as the throng thins out along the sidewalk. Each competitor has his own pace, a fingerprint. Some will finish while others will not. You settle into a natural trot and feel the explosion of your pulse, your gasping breaths. Your legs feel turbine strong and even a series of stomach cramps seem like comrades in arms. You are a scarred but stubborn soldier, still pushing on, while Jason is lost somewhere at the head of the pack.

"For luck," Donna said.

You run well. Her voice was a conspiratorial whisper. It embraces you, giving you hope.

The race grinds on, each second nearly a minute in length. You streak by runners who have slowed to a walk, others who have knelt by the side of the road to try to massage knots out of their leg muscles. Although you feel agonies of your own, cramps like angry fists and sweat that beads on your forehead or drips into your eyes, something marvelous in you has grown stubborn, even angry. You listen to each footfall, counting them like dollars you have earned and banked.

"For luck."

Luck has little to do with it, you decide, gritting your teeth and snorting. As you run, your mouth grows dry and cracked.

But suddenly you are astonished to see the race is nearly over. On this, the last street, you pass three more slowing runners, pushing on. The last block and there are two more racers ahead of you, a tall one in green and, incredibly, Jason. Something drives you into a sprint and the green foe falls behind. Then there is only Jason and the distant, approaching finish line. Jason is running hard, but you feel charged with victory, with . . . laughter. You pull up beside him, a rocket, and see the coming tape. As one, both of you enter the park just a few yards from the finish. You find yourself wondering if Jason knows who challenges him in the dying seconds of the race. Only a few yards now and you feel like Hermes. You lunge ahead of him and burst through the tape. You win.

There is no time to think of what you've done. Someone has taken your arm and is trying to make you walk, tugging on you, afraid you will collapse in blind exhaustion on the grass. "Keep walking. Don't stop," the mystery person says.

"For luck," Donna has said.

As your vision clears, there are people all around your intoxication, patting your back in some blurred congratulations. You scan the faces, looking for Donna. Or for Jason.

"Where are the spoils?" you sputter with drunken, dizzy glee.

But no one answers you and no one seems to laugh.

For a time you are left alone to wander around the park, trying still to catch your breath, your hands on your hips and your legs trembling so much you feel they will let you down. The cramps are easing now and you slowly find your way back to the centre of things.

Everything seems confused. Jason is putting his jacket on, not looking in your direction. Donna bursts out of the crowd, then rushes towards him. Time stops, it seems. In a moment, someone, Donna or you or Jason, will have to turn away. When Donna embraces Jason, your stomach goes vaguely sour. Suddenly you feel stupid and twisted. When you reach for the medal Carol has given you, you discover it is missing, has been lost along the route.

Above Donna's gleaming hair, Jason looks at you. You are instantly connected by something sad. At that moment, the way things were before the race seems gone forever.

Then someone you hardly notice, obscured by your unhappiness, gently takes your arm. "They want to present the trophy."

You nod and let yourself be led away.

DANCE

The final short story featuring Phillip Barrett as a main protagonist travelled a circuitous route to the summer 1988 issue of Grain. *My submission of* DANCE—*then called* Four-Oh-One—*to a literary magazine called* Waves *was accepted by editor Joan Fern Shaw. There was some editorial back and forth that I was not used to in the literary magazine circuit. The changes were minor, the most major one being a suggestion that I change the title.* Dance *was the result.*

Time passed, as it often did with literary magazines, between acceptance and publication. One issue before my story was to appear, I received a letter from Joan telling me that Waves *would cease publishing, that my story would not appear before the magazine's last issue. She encouraged me to send it elsewhere and explain in my covering letter that the story had been scheduled for publication with* Waves. *I was not about to give up on the* story and began to send it out again. Grain *accepted it and it appeared in the summer 1988 issue.*

While Dance *was the last short story with Phillip Barrett as the main protagonist to be published in a literary magazine, I wrote two others but soon decided they didn't have much to say that had not been thematically said before. I had also begun to move away from the exclusive second person viewpoint that I had hoped would broaden point of view in fiction. I had not intended it to be a trademark. Later, though, I embarked on a novel about Phillip Barrett, written primarily in the second person,* The Last Light Spoken, *a coming of age story predating his misadventures as a romantically troubled teenager or adult. With a novel in mind as a conclusion to stories about Phillip Barrett, the two new stories found themselves in my drawer of never to be published material.*

Ultimately these decisions were mine. But they were also the response to a paradigm shift in literary magazines. The radicalism of my second person viewpoint technique—which I had not considered radical at all—began to butt up against a growing conservatism in short fiction that, in my opinion, has accelerated more and more into the new millennium. I have even encountered editors unfamiliar with interior or dramatic monologues and a wide variety of other experiments in viewpoint. The history of the development and use of various narrative points of view, in my personal view, is on a voyage to where such points of view—beyond the extraordinarily conventional—may end up extinct.

I have never conceived of a creative writing project—book-length or otherwise—with an intended target for its publication. I do not try to imagine a convention in my audience and write to please it. Quite the opposite. I conceive of the story idea and the way in which it should be written, then try to find a magazine or publisher that will print it in that form. Each story, long or short, has its own way of wanting to be written. For the most part, though, I still maintain my stories need to be written in ways that reflect the way we live our lives—in the past, present and future tenses, and in the first, second and third persons. If something must be written chronologically backwards to make its point, as my memoir Every Wolf's Howl did, well that's the way it must be written. And, thanks to publishers like Freehand Books, that's also the way it can be published.

The new millennium has many more rules in writing than there were when I began publishing thirty and forty years ago, many more rules too than when Dorothy Parker wrote But The One On My Right nearly a century ago. And these rules are purveyed in the context of some great new espoused digital "freedom" to be creative, to reimagine. Ironic really. The people who maintain we now live in an era of more creative freedoms make this assertion in the most narrow of creative times, in my opinion.

But we don't get to choose what we write, or in which genre, or according to a particular paradigm's rules. The stories choose all this for us. While publishing our work *may have a myriad of regulations around the publishing process, writing the work does not. And one new digital freedom—self-publishing that is affordable—permits us to find small pockets of readers who read as some of us write: outside of literary locales defined by too many rules.*

DANCE

GET DOWN AND BOOGIE, BABY. Night Flight. At midnight, here on your superstar station.

Your grin is a grimace and your fingers ache on the wheel.

Watch that driving. A heavy snowfall warning has been issued for all of southern Ontario. Accumulations of up to twenty-five centimeters overnight.

Twenty-five centimeters translates into ten inches. A lot of snow. And shit, the stuff that fell this morning is already drifting across the pavement. What's metric for the danger of drifting snow, for anything that drifts or wanders? Nothing fits in metric. You'd walk a mile for a Camel?

The snow swirls crazily in your headlights, white flakes turned black in the glare. The men who look after the MacDonald-Cartier Freeway have already been through spreading salt and sand, but you drive at fifty miles per hour, holding the wheel in both sweating palms. Again and again, you glance at the sideview mirror, watching for traffic behind you, preparing to overtake you in a fog of snow, salt and highway filth. After five years of travelling this highway during the winter, you are convinced no one ever passes on the bare spots; they wait for curves and slippery sections. You enjoy conclusions of this nature, holding dear those incidents when God, if He exists, seems to act out of spite.

Alone in a car on the highway in winter, you're conscious of the meaning of loneliness. Sometimes you say the word aloud just to hear its sound, to emphasize your acknowledgement of its existence.

"Loneliness."

Your voice is buried by the babble on the radio and you reach out to switch it off. Suddenly you can hear the hum of the car's engine and the whisper-kiss the tires make on the slushy pavement.

The Cougar is part of the mystery of the night, a shadow all around you except where its B-52 cockpit spurts brilliant green light. It runs by itself. You are permitted to have only the wheel and a foot on the accelerator.

Outside the world is black or grey. The line that should separate winter sky from winter earth is indistinct, except when cars approach and pass on the other side of the median. You are submerged in a horizonless universe and the Cougar swims like an otter, backwards and forwards, making sport of your fear. One fierce tug on the wheel and, yes, it could somersault through the highway ink, emerging with laughter, unscathed.

How long ago was it that you enjoyed driving? How long ago was it that you were not intimidated by winter, by night, by a lonely and dangerous highway? When did you last not believe you were at the mercy of a powerful automobile and drivers who hurry through your life in careless distraction? Thousands of miles ago perhaps. So many comings and goings. Hundreds of them. Going to see your sons or to merge briefly with a woman, then coming back again.

Startling lights appear in the mirror by your left window and you grip the wheel even more tightly. A truck passes you, blinding you with blowing snow. You imagine the driver, plaid shirt and big workman's hands, CBing his selfish neglect all over the countryside. Cursing, you slow down to let him go by quickly, or else he will suck you along in his velocity.

Mary, your ex-wife, was annoyed that you wanted to see the boys. She was having a party and your time together would have to be brief. She didn't want them upset over such a short visit. You showed up anyway and refereed an argument. Danny wanted to go to a proper restaurant and Tony wanted to go to McDonald's. You taught them to toss a coin and tried to explain that someone has to win and someone has to lose. Your fatherhood lesson didn't cut any ice with Mary. She reminded you it wasn't your weekend, made it plain that one hundred and forty miles for a three-hour visit was selfish on your part, especially when Tony carries on so much after you leave to go home again.

Home again. Where's home to a man who leaves pieces of himself scattered everywhere?

Danny won the toss. Then, on the way to the restaurant, exercised his five-year old prerogative and changed his mind. Now he wanted pizza.

"Whaddyuh think, Tony?" you asked.

"Yeah! Pizza!"

They were brothers again.

"Ten years from now you guys will come in here all the time," you told them in the pizzeria, trying to get closer to them, trying to promise a future far different from the present and all its rejection.

The tablecloth was plaid and Danny traced the design with a dirty fingernail. You sniffed pepperoni odors which, by the time you left, would cling to your clothing, hitching a ride.

"Yup," you said. "After school you'll be down here. On Friday and Saturday nights."

"Why, Daddy?" Danny asked.

"Why?" stumbled his brother, Little Sir Echo, who had no questions of his own.

"Because you'll still love pizza and you'll be chasing girls."

"Chasing girls?"

"Yeah. Finding yourself a girlfriend."

"I already have a girlfriend," Danny said.

Tony nodded. Even Tony knew it was true.

"Is she nice?" you asked.

"Sure," Danny replied. "But she tries to make me mad. She teases the other boys to make me mad. It's lucky I know what she's doing."

"Danny knows," Tony said, his blue eyes wide and proud.

"Her name's Annie," Danny said.

"That's a nice name," you told him, approaching the edge of tears the way you always do when your sons are growing up and you've been away from the transition.

Now, in your car, you smile as best you can, believing it's really possible Danny, at five, knows more about women than you do. At least he knows when not to care or when he shouldn't be fooled.

Another drive, a few years ago, when you would have been happy with Danny's confident knowledge. Angela. For days, she had made light of everything you felt and, worse, everything you wanted to feel.

You and Angela, further west on this very highway. It was summer then, August, and the sun was sticky hot. Angela had stayed three weeks and she was leaving Toronto Airport to go back to the west coast. Someone on the radio then, singing a tortured song. *Baby, you talk of pain, it's all you ever do. Why can't you remember that I've been there too?* You were relieved that she was going back. For three weeks, she had wrestled with and laughed at your elastic, distended emotions. You promised yourself, when she parted from you at the gate, that you would never see her again.

This time, during the drive back home alone, you were ashamed because you had been so passive with her, because you'd allowed her to braid your frayed feelings into a cat-of-nine-tails she could beat you with. That time, the drive was terrifying and exhilarating. Eight-five and ninety. Each dotted line a cry of rage.

We should all be Clint Eastwood, you decide as the snow begins to thicken in the Cougar's headlights. Now there's a man more believable than you. He's real. He's not passive. No one gives him shit at the company water cooler. No one pushes him around. And the women, well, they don't cause him any pain.

Clint Eastwood would drive through the building snowstorm at eighty miles per hour. But you ease up on the accelerator and watch the needle drop to forty.

The car cannot always be trusted. Last time, going up to see the kids, it coughed, then died along the freeway, barely ten miles from your destination. A cold Saturday night. You managed to pull it over to the shoulder where it wouldn't start, in spite of your anger. Finally, you climbed out and went around to the front where you lifted the hood and peered into its vitals. In the darkness, though, there was nothing but a cold, stupid engine staring back at you.

So you walked along the edge of the road, cold because your gloves were on the coffee table at home, and each time a transport went by, you shuddered in the malicious wind it created. Shortly, you came upon a farmhouse in the middle of a field. You crossed the ditch, crunching through the hard crust of January snow, scaling fences and puffing with the exertion.

The man who answered your knock was dressed in coveralls over tattered longjohns. He mistrusted you at first, until you politely explained what you were doing at his door in the middle of his Canadian wilderness. Embarrassed by your apologies, he hurried you inside.

"Sure. Happens all the time. Call a tow truck."

"Look, I'm really sorry about this."

"Yeah, yeah. No sweat."

Clint Eastwood, you remember now, would have handled it better. Not so polite, not so defeated.

You recall there was something too damned Canadian about that house. It was stuck out there in the middle of a forever of snow, an igloo with a television tower. Hockey Night in Canada was on, a grudge match between Les Canadiens and the Maple Leafs.

Everything's trapped, it seems to you now. You on the inside of the Cougar. The man in his Canadian winterscape house. This country in its peculiar hemisphere.

Now you round a bend in the highway and come upon two tractor trailers lumbering off the shoulder onto the pavement. Carefully, you ease the car into the lefthand lane and go by them, regretting the need to do so because soon they'll reach their normal speed and pass you in reply, burying you in snow and fear.

Last winter on highway 400. Remember that one? The accident? Cars stopped all over the place, snow falling in their headlights, falling in persistent apathy on the man who was broken in half over the guardrails down the middle of the median. Six crowded lanes of suicidal drivers, red flares flickering in the storm, warning everyone of automobile and human debris littering the pavement.

Or what about the winter before that? Twenty-eight vehicles. Yours was vehicle number twelve. The Nova's last gasp on 401. A truck jackknifed farther up the road.

In the driving snow, stupid cars ran into it, then more stupid cars collided with *them*, and so on down the line until the automobiles seemed nothing more than a string of gnarled wrecks.

You slow to thirty miles per hour and let the two tractor trailers go by. Then, when they are a safe distance ahead, you climb back to forty.

When you drive, you ask yourself if you know what you have given up or lost in this life, if you know what you haven't found yet. Then you ask the worst question of all: what if what you've lost and what you haven't found yet are the same thing?

When you drive, you think about your rejection by Danny and Tony. How can they be content to be fatherless? Why don't they want you to be more than a favorite uncle, or a cartoon on television that can be switched off and forgotten as soon as a re-discovered toy turns up under the sofa?

And when you drive, you come upon a lost procession of women and you wonder why they are attracted by the outlaw in you, then discouraged when you give yourself up to their posse? In the end, you've decided, the things which initially entice them also drive them away. A man looking for joy or despair is only interesting if he does not find what he seeks.

You must learn to be less passive in life. As a hero, you'd like to take control. Just once, having conceived the idea during other 401 journeys, you'd like to lie down on the bitter asphalt and shape the life of some other unwitting traveler who would drive over your intruding carcass like so much wasted wildlife.

Why the hell not? As the song goes, are you the dancer or the dance?

You park your car on the shoulder, the lights extinguished, the engine running. You walk into the passing lane and lie down in the deepening snow, waiting for the next car with its fate-tricked driver, snowflakes falling on your face and into your open mouth, that melody about the dancer and the dance repeating itself in your memory. You can tell what you are. Here in the passing lane, snow-obscured but black, you are certain you are the dance.

The oncoming car, the lights on your flesh, your arms over your face in a pathetic attempt to lessen the blow, the swish of the snow under his tires, the scratch of the metal as he swerves into the snowbank along the median, the strangled gasp as his engine dies.

You leap to your feet and run from the road. You climb into your car and turn on the lights. The red-faced crazy-mad driver lurches across the highway to do with his bare hands what he has avoided doing with his car.

"Jesus Christ!" he screams, grabbing at the door handle, his fingers slipping away as you spin from the shoulder onto the asphalt.

At first, as you pull away from him, he runs along beside you, a man with no face but anger, nondescript ski jacket, a quiver in his obese belly.

You laugh. If there is ultimate rejection, it is

rejection by death. Hysterical, crazy with life, you have been the dance.

Barry Grills

EXPECTED FOR DINNER

EXPECTED FOR DINNER *was a significant departure for me from the voice of my previous stories. The story, written from an elderly female's point of view, seemed to require a more traditional approach. Elderly was a stage in life I believed was connected to a voice that wasn't experimental and the story turned on the confusion between new ways and old ways of doing things, which I wanted to present from the point of view of the traditional.*

The story was accepted in 1988 by Alistair MacLeod, then fiction editor of The University of Windsor Review. *When the story appeared in the Volume 21, Number 1 issue, the copy that arrived in the mail contained a cheque for fifteen dollars and an apologetic note from Mr. MacLeod for the small amount. Blamed were declining grants. Compared to thirty years later, when authors often receive no payment, fifteen bucks was fifteen bucks. Yet it was a far cry from the one hundred dollars I was paid for my first story that appeared fifteen years earlier in 1973.*

In 2003 Alistair MacLeod and I would encounter one another again when I, as chair of The Writers' Union of Canada, drove him to the Writers' Trust Margaret Laurence Lecture he was presenting one evening. Then, at the last minute, due to an organizational error, I was nominated to introduce him to the assembly. During the drive, I told him about his note and the cheque for fifteen dollars that had accompanied my story to my doorstep. By then, in the very early days of the new millennium, we knew how tough things were going to get for writers and their incomes. The esteem with which writers had been treated thirty years earlier, as a matter of course, was already dramatically in decline. Despite his own personal success, Alistair MacLeod admitted this was so.

EXPECTED FOR DINNER

BY ELEVEN-THIRTY IN THE MORNING, Maude Griffin had all the burners on the Moffat range glowing red beneath four different-sized pots. She squinted at the clock on the stove to verify that she was on schedule, then gave up when the tiny hands blurred before her eyes. She glanced instead at the larger face on the kitchen clock a few feet higher. Time in a flower basket, a Christmas gift. The hands were shaped like the stems and petals of tulips and they moved slowly from one flowered number to another, the whole horticultural morass set in a basket, real wicker. Gaudy when you actually got down to it. Mrs. Osborne down the hall, who felt safe among provocative things, had given it to her. Poor Mrs. Osborne! The louder an object was, the more it kept her from the silent gray of death. She was a woman with a blaring television, with walls of brilliant paisley, and she could panic at a whispered voice, as if it was enough to condemn her to the end of her days.

Maude didn't visit her much anymore because she set everyone to shouting. You couldn't help it. It was like entering the fun house at the fair. Eventually you became part of the entire performance, an integral fixture in some kind of calamity. Finally, when you left to go back to your own apartment, the quiet, the relief, the peace all settled down on you like a weight. It might have been a golden burden, this peace, but by the time Mrs. Osborne got done with you, it was heavy just the same.

Maude stood before the stove and watched steam come out of the boiling potatoes and carrots. Leftover gravy thinned itself out in another pot while a can of peas had begun to simmer in yet another. The meat was in the oven, a roast beef which had seemed to last forever. Perhaps her company would help her finish it off. She'd been eating it more than a week, working away at it like a chunk of marble, whittling it down to size meal after meal. You knew you lived alone when it took so long to eat a roast. If Sidney had been still alive, it would've been gone in half the time. Whatever you said about the old fart, he'd always enjoyed his food.

Maude was eighty-three. It was old age, the real

thing. There were so many days marked by pain because of her arthritis. She wasn't a person who felt sorry for herself and so she didn't actually count the days in which she suffered, but she knew instinctively how often they took place. Most days now, each joint aching as if it had broken away from her well-being and had turned on her in vengeance.

She'd stayed in bed until nearly ten this morning, even though she knew they were coming for dinner. Shameful. But the pain had kept her there. She was a woman more used to rising at six a.m. You couldn't do otherwise if you were a country girl. A farm could slip into failure if you spent too much time in bed. And she'd lived on a farm until she was nearly seventy. Up early every day and going about your business. In Maude's view, that was the real difference between the country and the city. Late was the word which best described the city. Late to bed, late to get up, late for work, late buses and trains, late payment of what was owed. But not when you worked on the land. There, everything was early, retiring at night, getting up in the morning, the bills, the chores, the hard work.

So, this morning, she lay in bed, wide awake with humiliation, under no real pressure to get up but thinking she would anyway because it was the *right* thing to do. Right was a good enough reason. Rightness was clear and, at eighty-three especially, one yearned for things to be clear.

Maude turned everything on the stove down and left

the kitchen. She eased by the dining room table which she'd already set. She hadn't known how many settings to prepare. Her grandson hadn't said how many would be coming, all the kids, just his step-daughter or simply he and his wife. Or if he'd said, she couldn't remember. That was the hard part. These days she was never *sure*. She missed a memory which didn't let her down, longed for her younger days when she had had a table for six, herself, Willy, his wife, all three kids. She'd like to see the kids. There were only a handful of women in the building with great grandchildren. As far as she knew she was the only one on this floor.

She'd put out cloth napkins, the ones Willy and his wife had given her for Christmas last year. Willy's wife would be suspicious; this would be the first time she'd taken them out of their box. Their creases were as sharp as a razor. Maude had never used cloth napkins in her life, just the paper ones on special occasions. When she'd opened the present last Christmas, she hadn't known what they were at first. That was another thing about getting old. People's gifts weren't something you needed. They were something else, something you'd never thought about, something which revealed they didn't know you well enough anymore to know what you required. And somehow they seemed to be part of a package, colour-coordinated. The napkins on her table now, for instance, matched the dining room drapes perfectly. Maybe modern women kept a little notebook for such things: *dining room drapes, navy blue, napkins to match*?

Willy still liked home-made preserves. Even as a boy, he had. So the table was clustered with jars of pickles, chili sauce, mustard relish, beets. Not that pickling was the same these days. For Maude, some of the legitimacy was lost because she no longer grew her own ingredients. Now it was all one step removed; she bought everything at the market.

She wondered if their car might be pulling up outside, so Maude moved, without actually thinking about it, to the heavy sliding doors, tugged one open and stepped outside onto the balcony. It was already warm, an old-fashioned July day.

The street was deathly quiet. She stood there for more than five minutes but not one car drove past. Maude lived three floors up, more or less in the middle of the apartment block, if you didn't count the basement. A senior citizens building, subsidized housing. Even here, on this very balcony, the superintendent had talked proudly about the view. Though she'd kept her opinion to herself, she'd thought his remarks were nonsense. All you could see were buildings. The superintendent had a beer belly. A drinker who thought endless buildings constituted a view was probably a fool. Space. Now that was what made a view. Openness, distance, a land taking shape like a quilt, a landscape pattern so complex only God could've designed it. Maude knew all there was to know about glancing towards the horizon. A view didn't have anything manmade in it. What men constructed somehow went weak in the foundation and, as such, it simply couldn't last. That was the difference. No matter how hard they tried, men could not be God.

Maude lingered on the balcony a few minutes longer, then discovered herself rubbing her hands together, trying to soothe the endless ache in her joints. She was not a woman to cry, not even when her body seemed completely enveloped by pain. Accordingly, she didn't weep now. Instead, she went back inside and tried to find something to do.

When the potatoes and carrots were done, Maude drained them into the sink. The steam rose like a geyser. Willy and his family were late and she'd begun to fret about it. What to do with dinner? It was after twelve now. And underneath it all, she was afraid she'd gotten something wrong. He'd said Sunday when he called. She was sure of it.

She could hear his voice. "We thought we'd pop in for a short visit Sunday."

Yes, he'd said Sunday. And today was Sunday.

"Why don't you come for dinner?" Maude had said.

Willy hesitated. She could tell he felt cornered. Maude could pick it up in people's voices, their reluctance to be forced into the commitment of a more involved or longer visit.

"We don't want to put you to any trouble," he said finally. Willy had always been clever, shrewd, polite in his rejection. Even as a boy, he had been able to squirm out of commitments.

"It's no trouble at all," she replied.

"Okay," he'd said finally. "Dinner sounds nice."

And that had been that.

But here it was past noon and they hadn't arrived yet and maybe, just maybe, her memory was playing tricks on her again.

Maude mashed the potatoes, rinsed the masher, them mashed the carrots. What now? She spooned them into bowls, When she glanced at the tulip clock, it didn't help her much, just told her it was twenty after twelve.

Held up in traffic perhaps. On Sunday? An accident maybe. She shuddered. God, no, there'd been enough of that already. Jesse dead decades before his time.

Just late getting away from Carl and Jean's in Toronto. She could remember the arrangements now. He'd explained it on the phone.

"We'll be going to Mum and Dad's for the weekend, but we'll pop in on our way back to Kingston," he'd said.

Encouraged by her recollection of his words, Maude put the bowls in the oven and turned the dial to warm. That way, dinner'd keep for a while at least.

She returned to the living room and sat down in the easy chair near the balcony doors. There, she could perch on the edge of the chair and watch the street for Willy's car. In the fabric of an apron she couldn't remember putting on, she wrapped her aching knuckles and tried to knead the pain away.

The telephone rang. It was Olive Breckenridge from the fourth floor.

"Maude," she said, "I was about to hang up."

"There's nothing gained in breaking your neck to get to the phone."

Reproofed, Olive sighed. "I'm not taking you away from lunch, am I?"

"No, I haven't eaten yet."

"Good heavens," said Olive. "It's nearly one o'clock. You aren't under the weather, are you?"

"My arthritis is kicking up, that's all. Otherwise I'm fine."

"I thought you might come up for tea and cake."

"I can't," Maude said. Then she explained about Willy and how he was late and how they'd left Carl and Jean's in Toronto and were probably tied up in traffic on that *dreadful* Four-oh-one. "Everything's in the oven," she said. "If they don't come soon, it'll be ruined."

She hadn't wanted to tell Olive so much. It wasn't any of Olive's business. Yet, she'd gone ahead and said too much. She wished she could just hang up.

"Well, I suppose there's nothing else to do but wait," Olive told her. "Young people these days don't have the consideration we had. They're *always* late, *always* keeping you waiting."

"I know," Maude said half-heartedly.

"They don't realize how important it is to be punctual, what an inconvenience it is to keep people waiting."

Well-worn themes. Olive was from the city and it was just as well. If she'd had to plough a field the way Maude had, the job would never have been done. Olive went over and over each personal furrow, ploughing it to death.

"I must go, Olive," Maude said. "I'd better check on the oven. I don't want everything to dry out."

"Okay, Dear. I'll talk to you later."

"We'll have tea tomorrow. Down here, maybe."

"Sure. Call me."

After she hung up, Maude peered out the window again. Two cars were now parked on the gravel shoulder and she couldn't remember how long they'd been there. Cloud was filling the sky and the sunlight was fading. The weather came in from the west; maybe there'd been a rainstorm in Toronto. For a long time, she watched the street, waiting for her guests, hoping nothing was wrong.

At one-thirty, she turned the oven off. It had occurred to her now that they weren't coming at all, that something had gone wrong. It was probably something ordinary, something in the realm of the harmless or unforeseen, but she was still concerned. Maude didn't like to worry about bad things, accidents, deaths; she was afraid worry made them come true.

She went to her bedroom and laid down. Under normal circumstances, she would have been napping by now. It was part of the puzzle sleep had become in her life. All day, she could nap and doze, sometimes half a dozen times. Then, at night, when a person really wanted to sleep, she just laid awake and suffered. Was it a function of age? Was that the final confusion? Were aged humans transformed into nocturnal beings, disoriented for the remainder of their days?

Maude slipped into a shallow sleep.

She dreamed about Sidney who had died a year and a half ago. It wasn't a deep dream. It didn't take her entirely out of reality. No, it tugged her into that ambivalent state between sleep and wakefulness where the conscious part of your mind wrestles with the unconscious, where truths are argued against distortions, where unreality debates violently with reality.

In the dream, she was young again, hardly more than a little girl, the little girl she had been when Sidney had come to take her for his wife. She was outside in the garden on their farm and it was hot and sunny. She could feel a patch of sweat at her shoulder blades, nothing unseemly, but an odourless perspiration which mingles so well with the inexplicable satisfaction one feels sometimes when one is working with one's hands. Hatless, she was weeding the garden. It was a fine garden, almost brilliant in its early summer greenery. When she leaned back on her heels to briefly rest, she surveyed its entirety. It seemed to stretch on for miles towards a distant horizon. Yet, even in its largeness, her garden didn't seem unworkable, an impossible challenge. No, it was simply fine and wonderful, an indescribable masterpiece of creation.

Then Sidney was there beside her. He stood in the bare earth nearby and rested his hand on her shoulder.

"It's a wonderful garden, Maude," he said.

"Yes," she whispered without looking up at him. "It is, isn't it?"

Then she came awake. Because the dream was all a

terrible lie.

Lying on her bed, she felt a deep, irresistible anger. And she was ashamed as well. How could her sleeping mind transform Sidney into someone he had never really been? How could her mind forget that he had been a miserable little man with a streak of cruelty much larger than his size?

When Carl, her oldest son, had been barely growing inside her, Sidney had wanted him destroyed. He hadn't wanted the being who would eventually become his first son. No reason. Just cruelty. Sidney had always refused to explain himself. Four sons. Eventually, four sons, each one treated so differently. Carl, denied everything by his father, yet making do on what his mother could secretly acquire for him. Then Nathan, another young workhorse to bear the load of the farm. Edgar. He looked like Sidney in a larger frame and he earned liberties because of the resemblance, Sidney's favourite until Jesse came along. Then Jesse. Spoiled as if, with each son, Sidney softened against them until, at last, some streak of kindness broke free of its bonds. Jesse was sickly. She was told, just after his birth, that he had a heart ailment. But he grew and survived. Until . . .

Sidney. Their life together had been so much longer than she really wanted it to be. His randy fathering of sons until, finally, she found the strength to turn him away for good.

"Go find yourself another woman if you want," she'd said. "I don't care."

If he did, she never knew it. She didn't hear a word about anything like that.

Back then, breakfasts began at the crack of dawn before everyone embarked on his chores. A half egg for Carl and a half egg for Nathan, even with a hen house full of eggs. Then, when Sidney left the table and headed for the barn, she'd cut her eggs in half and give the pieces to her sons.

Everyone grew, older and up, and one by one her sons went off to make lives of their own. Sidney stayed behind. A dangerous bout of pneumonia nearly killed him but, in the end, it didn't even shorten his life. When her mother died, she inherited another farm. It split their finances in two and, thank God, their incomes would remain separate forever, his farm, her farm. She sold it after a year went by and held the mortgage herself. There was at least a financial independence. Sidney couldn't touch that money the way he couldn't touch *her*.

They moved into the city after they sold his farm. The large Christmases of sons and daughters-in-law and the quarrels and laughter of children would now be gone forever. Sidney was ten years older than her. He began to lose his mind, not in a mean way which was a blessing, but in a humiliating confusion which only increased the load of her responsibilities. He even began to try to bed her again. She had to lock the door. Or else he wandered off somewhere and she'd have to search the streets to find him and bring him home.

Her sons finally gathered one Sunday in September.

Carl, as the oldest, was the spokesman, though all four boys were united in their mission.

"Dad has to go to a nursing home," he said.

Maude argued at first. She'd considered the same thing herself from time to time but wouldn't accept the high costs.

"The old man can afford it," Jesse said.

Maude shot him a dirty look. "The old man" was not a phrase she tolerated from her sons, regardless of how Sidney had behaved for most of his life. They all knew her feelings about it.

"Sorry," Jesse muttered.

"It'll use up all his money," said Maude, speaking to Carl again.

'He doesn't need it anyway, Mum. What's Dad going to do with his money the shape *he's* in?"

"Leave it to his sons, that's what. He'll leave it to me and I'll divide it up among you. He owes you. A nursing home will eat up your inheritance."

The debate went on much of the afternoon, but in the end her sons won their point. It was for *her*, because she deserved a better life. Though it took some time, Maude finally understood that they were trying to give her more peaceful circumstances. It would be ungracious not to accept their gift.

She visited him every other day at the nursing home. She didn't know why. It wasn't love. A side of her had always despised Sidney, even when he grew less cruel as he aged, even when his meanness and her hatred of it were transformed into a sleepy kind of tolerance for one another. In her secret moments, she supposed she would have divorced him had she lived in more modern times. That was the way things were done today. But no, she had been raised to believe a woman didn't just walk out, regardless of her unhappiness. One learned to accept one's lot, whether it was what you'd really wanted or not.

All of that had now changed. Today's world was much different. Oh sure, her sons had stuck with their wives. Their wives had stuck with them. She'd done *something* right, she supposed. But with her grandchildren, it was another matter. Willy, divorced once. Two other divorces in the family. And all of them so young to be admitting their unfortunate failure. Yet, even so, with hardly any mourning, they went on with life. Maude considered them careless, a secret judgment she would never have passed on to them. But *their* children. What about them? Fathers and step-fathers, mothers and step-mothers, a kind of parental porridge she knew must be sticky and hard to digest.

Sometimes it just didn't make sense. Sometimes just looking out the window, she felt a deep wash of confusion come over her. There was so much scurrying out there, so much running around, back and forth, back and forth. *They* all called it work. But it wasn't work, not really. It seemed to be nothing more than frustration. Like mice, they scurried along the baseboard of life, dashing here when the fear got them, then in some other direction when it reared up at them somewhere else again. Not work. Maude suspected work, real work, would have been a helpful antidote.

She'd gone to the nursing home the morning Sidney died. He'd passed away in his sleep in the middle of the night, the nurse told her. She'd been inwardly angry at the news. Sidney had never suffered and that didn't seem fair. But that was only part of her anger. The remainder she reserved for herself because somehow one didn't alleviate one's own suffering by wishing it on someone else, regardless of how richly they deserved it.

They pulled back the plastic from his face. Ninety-two and hardly a trace of shrunkenness, no indication that he had been at all damaged by the cruelty of his youth and the losses he had suffered because of it. Strange, but you expected there to be some mark on his face, maybe like the mark God placed on Cain, some physical manifestation of love squandered or lost because you were too stupid to accept it, maybe even too stupid to really need it. Sidney could've had more than he'd had in life. Yet you couldn't tell it from his face which, in death, seemed only to sleep. Is that what they meant when they said ignorance was bliss? She supposed it was. Losses aren't losses if you don't know you've lost them.

Maude glanced at the perpetually humming alarm clock on the night table by her bed. Nearly three o'clock.

She suspected they weren't coming for dinner after all. She wished they'd found a way to telephone.

Maude didn't get out of bed. She thought she should, even thought she *would*. But she didn't move, giving in instead to an uncharacteristic laziness and the ache in her swollen joints which gobbled up her energy.

She had resolved today not to think about Jesse, but now she couldn't help it. Giving in to his memory, Maude accepted its inevitability. Hardly a day went by without some recollection of her youngest son.

Cancer.

Not much of her life remained, yet had there been a great deal ahead of her, nothing would ever equal the hurt of Jesse's loss. It wasn't that it was Jesse. Carl or Nathan or Edgar too. If any of them had died ahead of her, it would have represented the most severe agony of her life as well. In the end, though, it had been Jesse, her youngest. Not the ailing heart. Just cancer. Death monster. Some greedy child-demon which devoured human flesh.

She'd been in the hospital every day for his dying. She'd sat on the edge of his bed and imagined she could suck the cancer out of him with the force of her stubborn will. She'd failed, of course. Jesse just kept on fading, day after weary day. He was terrified to die, sulky one day, angry the next, terrified again a day later. And she couldn't *do* anything.

God must have been angry with her. Only His anger could take a woman's son before He took the woman herself.

Now Maude dozed again, ensnared by the pain of loss. It didn't throb like her arthritic-agonized joints. It just swallowed her up and held her in a kind of claustrophobic embrace. She could sleep with it and carry it with her wherever she went. Like a shadow, she often thought.

When she awoke later, she made herself get up. Her waking thought had been concern for Willy and his family. She had decided to call Toronto.

"They left about an hour and a half ago," Jean explained.

Puzzled, Maude didn't say anything. Willy had said he was coming for dinner. And now it was four-thirty.

"Don't worry," Jean was saying. "The trip's about two hours. They should be there soon. And they said they were popping in to see you."

"It's just Willy said he'd be here for dinner."

"That's strange," Jean admitted. Then she laughed. "Today's young people," she explained. "Dinner for Willy means the evening meal, Maude. That's why they're not there."

"Oh," said Maude. "You mean they're coming for supper?"

"Sure. I'll bet that's what he meant."

Maude couldn't laugh the way Jean was laughing. It just didn't seem funny. Different words for different things. There wasn't anything funny about that. It just meant you were lost, that something had changed too much, that time had taken people away from one another and continued to drive them apart.

"Willy calls supper dinner. He calls dinner lunch."

"Well, that would explain everything," Maude murmured flatly.

"So they'll be there. Don't worry."

Jean chatted for five or ten minutes longer, but Maude didn't really pay much attention. She was too tired for that, in spite of her nap. Supper-dinner. Dinner-lunch. The world was lost to her.

Maude was at the window when the car drove up shortly after five. She stood there at the edge of the drape and watched as they unwrapped themselves from the little vehicle Willy now drove. Foreign car. Toyota, she guessed. Blue, the way the sky had been before the clouds came out of the west. Willy stretched, waved when he saw her at the window.

He didn't have his sons, just his wife and her daughter. Not my turn for the boys, Willy would probably say. And Maude would be mystified because his voice would hold no sadness. She would never have accepted the price he paid for divorce. Two days out of fourteen with his sons. Why didn't it feel for him the way it felt for her? His loss like her loss of Jesse. Only God could have taken one of her sons. If someone else had tried, she would have died to prevent it.

They were coming up the sidewalk. His new wife was pretty and refined. Her napkins matched her dining room drapes too. Somehow, you just knew it.

Maude went to the kitchen and turned the oven on. The meal would have to be re-heated. Goodness, it'd be as dry as an old chip.

She'd thought they were coming for dinner, but now it was going to be supper.

The door chimes rang and she headed towards the

door. There was a hollowness in her stomach, an awkward mixture of fear and sadness. In spite of all the past which bound them, she to her sons to their sons to their sons, she would be opening the door to strangers.

HALF NELSON

Written in the first person, HALF NELSON *was one of the few short stories I wrote in a straightforward use of what is perhaps the simplest and most straightforward of writing points of view. I wanted it to be a personal story and the first person—without the obfuscating alternative second person protagonist—seemed the way to go. The first person, to me, is the simplest of the "cock-eyed" voices a writer can employ; there is no temptation to stray from the restricted viewpoint into the minds of more than one character. It is also written in the conventionally more common past tense. I was tending towards less experimentation in my short stories by this time. My more experimental work, in the style I published in the 1970s, was also being consistently rejected.*

Nonetheless, NeWest Review *seemed to agree with my new approach and published* Half Nelson *in its April/May issue in 1989.*

Before I go any further, I should point out that during my short story days I apparently invented first names from a surprisingly short roster of candidates. The "Jesse" in this story bears no relationship to the "Jesse" who appeared in the previous story. It's only when we collect stories from a large span of time together that we discover all the "Jesses" and the "Erics" we felt the need to create as first names for characters when we'd forgotten using them earlier.

HALF NELSON

THE FIRST DISAPPOINTMENT that muggy July evening was that the boys had already been to a wrestling match. The news drained the air from my plans like a puncture in a party balloon.

"When was that?" I asked Eric, my older son.

"Last summer," he replied. "Mom and Jesse took us."

"That's right," Tommy, his brother, confirmed.

For the moment I didn't know what to say. It was difficult to get much of a handle on the depth of my disappointment. I was provoked, I guess, that something special had been taken away from me.

"Whatsamatter, Dad" asked Tommy.

"You didn't mention it, that's all. You didn't say a word last summer. How come?" I asked.

Eric shrugged his twelve-year-old shrug. "I guess we forgot about it."

"Well," I said at last. "I guess it doesn't matter. You'll enjoy yourselves anyway, won't you?"

When they nodded, I was only mildly reassured.

Silently, we resumed our shuffling progress towards the Burger King counter. It was busy tonight. The pale girl who would be serving us was gently pimpled and perspired in spite of the air conditioning. I could see her poking away at the silent cash register, inundated by a harsh clatter of activity. Every couple of minutes, she'd exhale a plume of air that whisked up her face to flick several strands of hair from her forehead. An instant later, they'd fall right back into place.

"Have a nice day," she said after every customer, her conjured smile vanishing as quickly as it had appeared.

Another chalky face. Modern youth. Why did they look like they were closing in on death? Too many problems? Too little sleep? Drugs? Hopelessness?

Such questions preoccupied me because Eric would be a teenager come January. As he and his brother were developing, they dragged me through the changes with them. Sometimes you don't notice the way the world progresses until you consider that the youngsters you love are growing up in it, that at some point they're going to live a life in it much different from your own.

"Dad . . . Dad? Can I have a milk shake instead of a Coke?"

"Sure. What kind?"

"Vanilla."

"What about you, Tommy?"

"Chocolate, please."

"Sold," I said, wanting to spoil them.

"Can I help you, Sir?" We'd finally reached the front.

I ordered and she repeated it into a microphone. Then she said. "Twelve forty-six, please."

"Hot, isn't it?" I mumbled, handing her a twenty.

She didn't hear me over the noise of the microphones echoing everyone's request, the loud chatter of children beseeching adults in the line-ups on either side and the slap of plastic trays against the counter.

Our food was sorted and loaded. She gave me my change.

"Thank you," I said, scurrying away from her "have a nice day", but I couldn't outrun it. It broke through the tunnel of noise behind me.

At a corner table, Eric and Tommy chose seats across from me. We unwrapped our food, decorating it with condiments we squeezed from plastic containers, and then began to eat.

It was unusual for me to be with the boys on a Wednesday night. Only on special occasions were we together in the middle of the week. The rest of the time, it was the every-other-weekend dictated by the terms of my divorce. With a wrestling match, we could make an exception. It was special occasion enough, whether they'd been the year before or not. I lived fifty miles away. They didn't have wrestling matches in *my* town. You came to the city for that.

Not that I was a wrestling fan. Not anymore, not since I'd grown out of it. I passed it up on television and I hadn't been to a live bout for twenty-five years, not since I was Eric's age. I wasn't here for me. Not this time.

It was just that I wanted the guys to enjoy it, something different for me to do with them. That's why I'd been disconcerted when I'd learned that Carol and Jesse had taken them last year, had managed to beat me to it. It wasn't Carol as much as Jesse, their surrogate father. He was the kind of man a divorced dad doesn't forget, pencil-thin moustache, jet black oily hair and the kind of eyebrows that look at you with a prevailing suspicion.

"Are your mom and Jesse wrestling fans?" I asked the boys as we ate.

"Jesse watches it on television every Saturday," Tommy replied.

"I guess that means he's a fan," I said.

"I don't know," Eric argued. "It's pretty phony. They fake it up a lot."

"Yeah," Tommy added. "One guy'll get thrown out of the ring onto the concrete and he looks hurt. And then he'll climb into the ring all of a sudden and kill the other guy. You wonder how he gets better so fast."

I had to grin. "Well, it's more fun at a live match. You get the noise of the crowd. You can see all the sweat. You can hear all the grunts and groans." I hesitated a moment, realizing I'd forgotten they'd been to a match before. "I've got front row seats, you know."

"Yeah?"

"Did you guys sit in front last year?"

They shook their heads, both of them together.

I wasn't surprised; front row wasn't Jesse's style.

"Anyhow, there's no point in going when you're a kid,

if you can't get into the front row," I told them. "Sometimes, if you're lucky, one of them comes down, hauls you into the ring and uses you to beat on his opponent."

Tommy's eyes were wide as saucers. Blue craters.

But Eric wasn't going for it. "C'mon, Dad," he said. "That didn't happen last year."

Found out, I managed to laugh. "Eat up, Guys," I said. "We don't want to be late."

I SUPPOSE I WAS TRYING to manipulate the past, to re-shape it a little. I wanted to take what had happened to me then and change ends, put myself on the giving side of the gift. Twenty-five years before, my Aunt Ida and Uncle Gus, childless all their marriage, had taken me to the matches. It was an occasion still discussed today. Although I'd had the time of my life, they had derived even more pleasure from watching me enjoy myself. That's what I wanted tonight. I wanted Eric and Tommy to have a night they would never forget so that I, as the benefactor, would know the gratification Ida and Gus must have felt.

I had to admit some of that evening long ago remained vivid in my memory. Little pieces of it clung to my experience like hairballs on a pair of woolen trousers. It wasn't that I could remember the names of the wrestlers. I couldn't always recall who were the bad guys and who represented the forces of good. I couldn't even have told you how many bouts were on the ticket. No, I remembered much less than that, only the little things. The sweat, some shallow lake on the canvas, and how a falling torso of more than two hundred and fifty pounds would slingshot beads of perspiration high into the air. My frustration that the referee never seemed to be looking when I desperately wanted him to be. The boos and catcalls from the crowd.

I was a believer then, of course. I was young enough for that, had so much left of my innocence. In *my* world, then, it was craziness to assume that adults faked their battles purely for my entertainment. I considered them too busy for that, too earnest, too constantly preoccupied by what they had to do to make a living. For me, adults never lied. They were committed to the truth. It made me, as a youngster, believe everything they said.

That night, a quarter of a century ago, became dangerous drama for me, a realistic demonstration of good against evil, housed in living flesh. I couldn't sit back and just watch. No, I made a spectacle of myself. I rose from my seat in the front row dozens of times, screaming at the referee to intercede when the bad guy was fighting dirty. Then I'd sit down and turn to my aunt and uncle, exasperated. It frustrated me that there might be failure in my sense of goodness and fairness.

Gus just laughed, of course, a hearty, joyful laugh. Maybe he was taking things too lightly, but I was too mesmerized by the gladiatorial battle to really care.

The featured bout was a tag team match boasting the dreaded Russian Raminsky Brothers. I despised Ivan Raminsky who was as evil as they come. He didn't disappoint me. I saw him reach down and pick up a balled wedge of tinfoil, a crumpled potato chip bag which a fan had tossed into the ring. I saw him hide it in his shorts.

I was up on my feet again, enraged, calling to the referee. "He's got tinfoil in his shorts, Ref, he's got tinfoil," my adolescent voice cracking in passion. I was desperate to ensure good's triumph over evil. In my mind, Ivan Raminsky was cheating. We had to put a stop to that.

But the referee didn't hear me. Or if he did, he ignored me.

Ivan Raminsky didn't. He turned a bearded, sweaty face to me, leered, then frowned in my direction.

"Sit down, you big stupide."

My mouth gaped in astonishment. Was he shouting at me? In slow motion, I crumpled into my chair, terrified, not knowing what else to do. Beside me, Ida and Gus were laughing so hard it approached hysteria.

"You could see his eyes sparkling," Gus said ever afterwards.

I FELT THIS MAGIC RECOLLECTION standing at my shoulder as I guided Eric and Tommy into the Memorial Arena. We could see the ring in the centre of the floor, spotlights beaming down on the canvas and the rope. It looked like some religious edifice, an ark, an altar, something sent down by the gods. And the noise, the building of excitement, chairs scraping against the concrete floor as people took their seats, their excited chatter echoing off the distant ceiling. We made our way, part of this stuttering mass of fans, up the aisles towards our chairs.

"This is where we play hockey," Tommy yelled over the babble of the crowd.

"I know," I replied. Had he forgotten I sometimes came to watch?

I glanced at him and then at Eric. It was clear they didn't see the ring in the same brilliant light as I did. They'd already glimpsed it here last year and, since then, they'd played hockey in this same old building. Familiarity breeding contempt.

I didn't know any of the wrestlers' names and I supposed it didn't matter. They were a thoroughly modern display, all jewels and wristbands of gold, studded gloves they pretended were weapons. And they presented an image of a more grotesque evil or a more anti-hero kind of goodness. Fortunately, I wasn't there for them. No, I was here to watch my sons, to exchange the youth I had been with the parent I was now, to give them what I had been given twenty-five years ago, and take in return the pleasure Ida and Gus had known.

But Eric and Tommy had too much of it figured out.

"Boy, *that* was phony," Eric said during the first bout, elbowing his brother to ensure that he had noticed.

"Yeah," Tommy murmured, shaking his head in disgust.

I began to feel the renewed ache of disappointment. It wasn't working out as I had planned.

I tried. I leaned forward at one point and bent in my

sons' direction. "See all that sweat on the canvas?"

"Yeah," Eric said. "Must be a quart of it."

But if they were intrigued by this observation, it didn't last very long. They just sat in their seats quietly, as if we were attending an opera or a ballet.

As far as I could tell, they didn't see this brash, titanic struggle as a battle between good and evil. It was merely some harmless entertainment. I felt foolish about this, embarrassed that I had seemingly promised them something important, then not delivered the goods. I hadn't realized wrestling was phony until I was a man. Eric and Tommy had discovered that fact already, although they were only children.

There was blood in the last bout that night. I didn't see how it happened or how it was done. I just saw a sweating giant with purple hair, holding his hands up to his face, then raging at the audience as blood trickled down his forehead from what appeared to be a series of cuts and gashes.

"Is that real blood, Dad?" Eric asked me.

"I don't know, Son," I replied.

It was true. I really couldn't tell for sure.

After it was all over, as we filed down the aisles with the rest of the crowd, heading for the exits, Eric touched my arm.

"You okay, Dad?"

"Yeah. Sure."

"You look kinda sad."

I draped my arms over my sons' shoulders. Afraid for their loss of innocence, it was all I could think of to do.

THE WINNING TICKET

My final published short story, THE WINNING TICKET *was written during the 1980s, although it did not appear until 2005 in Laurence Steven's anthology,* Outcrops: Northeastern Ontario Short Stories, *published by his Sudbury publishing house,* Your Scrivener Press. *By this time, I had given up writing short stories. I had switched to novels and had written three by this time, all of them differently experimental in nature. The "cock-eyed voice" remained clearly my voice but it spoke now in the longer form of the novel and in a memoir ultimately published by* Freehand Books, Every Wolf's Howl. *I had abandoned my experimental style in the short story, gradually turning to a more conventional approach.*

The Winning Ticket, *however, nearly appeared in a number of Canadian literary magazines. Most notably, after I handed it in for study and discussion as part of a week-long, intensive writing class with Leon Rooke, Leon told me he would be taking this story back to the west coast for consideration by his wife Constance, then editor of* The Malahat Review. *A couple of months later, the story came back with a brief, candid note from Leon explaining that his wife had not wanted the story, primarily because she was rather annoyed with* him.

Leon Rooke's writing class continues to have a profound effect on me as I work in the late stages of my writing career. He encouraged me, no matter what, to get the writing out. Worry about the editing and re-shaping later. He had perceived that I was sublimating my creative instincts. Since his sage advice, I have adhered to his maxim that smothering a story idea because it does not give birth to itself as a perfectly refined adult inhibits my creativity.

Years later I was able to convey to Leon the impact he had had on me in this regard. We were at a social engagement in Toronto and we embraced. Leon's advice to "get it out" rather than to wait for it to be perfect on the inside had changed everything for me and I had told him so. His powerful influence to correct a period of repressed writing before my workshop with him encourages me still, many years later.

In the years that followed, The Winning Ticket *remained, for me, the story that Leon had liked and had tried to get published. When the call from* Your Scrivener Press *came out for submissions, as a northern Ontario writer, I dug out the manuscript and sent it off. It was accepted and published, nearly two decades after it was initially written. This too explains the dated way in which winning lottery numbers are announced to the general public, a key element in the action of the story.*

THE WINNING TICKET

BEFORE ALL THE EXCITEMENT, it was just a typical day at *Moravia's F ne Italian Foods*. It was mid-afternoon, the lunch-time crowd long departed, too early yet for the kids from the high school, except for four senior girls skipping class who had wandered in at two-thirty for Cokes and chips 'n' gravy. The clock above the fridge, an old-timer with a black hour hand and a chipped minute hand, seemed sympathetic to the laziness of time. Its thin red second hand simply kept on moving, leaping from instant to instant, around a face that said *7-up*.

The people who were present sat in booths clustered at the front of the restaurant, as if they were part of the same group. Many of them were, but not all of them. The ones with the common bond kept looking at the clock.

"The bank closes at three-thirty," Johnny Stephens muttered, shaking his head in frustration.

In his early twenties, he was crammed into a booth with three others who shared his approximate age as well as his impatience. They were waiting for their paycheques so they could temporarily resolve an incestuous economy which bonded them together. They owed each other money. Johnny was in hock to a short companion sitting directly opposite him, to the tune of thirty bucks. Shorty, as he was called, sported a blonde attempted mustache and, to some people's amusement, had the real name Dale Evans. Shorty, in turn, owed Randy Carstairs twenty dollars. Randy sat beside him, across from Cindy Irwin, a startlingly obese young woman with a food stain of forgotten origin on the front of her sweatshirt, to whom Randy was indebted for a further twenty bucks. Although she was broke, Cindy, for her part, wasn't as preoccupied with the paycheque which hadn't arrived. Sometimes, when he wasn't being a jerk, she was in love with Randy. He was handsome in a starved or victimized sort of way and he didn't often sit in the same booth with her, so tantalizingly close.

"I hate this," Johnny was saying. "Payday's Friday. Here it is Tuesday and the bank's gonna close."

Everyone said "yeah" because there wasn't much else to say that hadn't been said already.

Fifteen minutes ago, Randy had gone back to the kitchen to see about the delay. When he had returned, he had reported Paul Symonds, the restaurant owner, was still working on the cheques and didn't appreciate the interruption.

So the waiting went on and on. A dozen employees now passed the time with coffee and a persistent drumming of their fingers on the scratched and aging Formica tables.

Perhaps a year ago, a former coworker had spread the news that being late with everyone's pay was probably illegal. But no one had paid much attention to him and nothing had ever been done about it. The coworker, his name and face forgotten, had been swallowed up in the anonymity of a larger than average employee turnover.

It wasn't that *Moravia's F ne Italian Foods* was in financial trouble. Not at all. The "i" might be missing from the sign outside, but business was brisk at meal times. Everyone knew Paul Symonds had money. He just paid late. Always had. The coffee, for those who waited, was free of charge, which everyone supposed was a kind of perpetual apology.

Outside on this January day, the street was banked with sooty snow. A major storm had hit a week ago. Immediately afterwards, the temperature had climbed and the deep powdery snowflakes had congealed into a dirty stew of sand and salt and litter. Now it was very cold, below zero, and the snowbanks were as hard as granite. Giant icicles hung from the roofs or from signs on the front of the stores along the street. When they fell, as they inevitably would, there would be a loud explosion.

Although the sun shone with that peculiar January brilliance, like an angled laser beam, you couldn't tell from inside the restaurant because the windows at the front were solid with frost, but for a six-inch section near the top of the glass. If you stayed inside long enough, you could forget what the day was like. Then, when someone opened the door, the cold and even a trace of sunshine seemed to burst inside, intent on startling everyone.

Inside it was hot and dry. The furnace, rattling and humming away in a cubbyhole in the basement, spat dusty insistent air through heavy metallic vents. On the ceiling, tired cardboard mobiles danced silently in the breeze, their gold paint aging into a wretched gray.

Moravia's F ne Italian Foods was like an old woman with traces of striking beauty. You suspected it had had a glorious past. At one time, the grimy red carpet had been rich and lush and thick. There was a salad bar in the corner but it had not seen a strip of lettuce in more than five years. It remained at its present location because no one knew what to do with it now that it was no longer in use. Yes, Moravia's had once been fancier, known for its fine dining. But now it simply served grub to patrons just looking for a cheap place to eat where they might feel at home. It was busiest at breakfast time. On the wall, near the cart containing the dirty dishes, was a hand-drawn sign promoting the breakfast special. Eggs with bacon or sausage, plus coffee and juice, for only $1.99. And on the tables, there was a full-color cardboard pyramid depicting something called pizza fingers. Someone had attached a white circular label and written "with fries - $2.95."

On this particular Tuesday, there was only one waitress on duty. The kids from the high school called her Happy Hilda because she was miserable by nature. Happy Hilda had now redefined the expression "slinging hash." It was an integral part of her legend that she could drop a plate of food from a height of three or four inches, and when it clattered on the table, not a single french fry was spilled. Today, Hilda had a cold. An empty Heinz Tomato Juice carton on a shelf behind the bar was already full to overflowing with soiled facial tissues.

Suffering, on the verge of complete despair, she dutifully refilled the coffee cups of those who waited to be paid, collected as they were in the front of the restaurant like cattle along a section of fence.

So it was, when the excitement broke out at five after three, there were twenty adults at the front of the restaurant, counting Hilda and her cold. There were the four girls from the high school, two men from a local surveying company, twelve restaurant employees and Calvin Smith, an elderly war veteran who lived in a small apartment on the second floor of Moravia's. There was also one child, the daughter of one of the dishwashers. Her mother had given her crayons and she drew colorful little designs on the back of a paper placemat. Her name was Amber, though there was nothing amber about her. Most of us imagine Ambers as tending to be blonde and pretty and slim. This one, five years old, was dark and fat and bearded by the grape jelly sandwiches her mother had served her for lunch.

Calvin sat at the bar, nursing a coffee and reading Monday's newspaper because the Tuesday edition wasn't out yet. He drank his coffee a tiny sip at a time, making it last. Calvin's coffee was not free and he had no claim on a paycheque. At fifty cents a cup, he was going to nurse it as long as he could.

"Lord Jesus!"

Calvin blurted the words during a lull in the conversation among the group of disgruntled employees.

Everyone turned to look at him.

"Lord Jesus!" he cried again, louder this time, as his body stiffened and he began to emerge from his slouch against the bar.

This time the four high school girls stopped tittering long enough to glance at him too. Dismayed at first, they fell to giggling, then whispering conspiratorially, as if they knew something about Calvin that he would *never* know.

"Whatsamatter, Cal?" Randy asked.

Calvin didn't answer. Frantically, he began to search the pockets of his jacket, the remaining half of a charcoal suit he had owned for fifteen years.

Randy shrugged and everyone went back to what they were doing. Calvin was old and grubby. It seemed to explain a lot.

"Holy Lord Jesus!"

"Watch your mouth," Happy Hilda snapped. "This is a restaurant."

That whipped everyone's head around again.

"Look at this," Calvin said to her. "Jesus, tell me I'm not going crazy."

"You're not going crazy, Calvin," Randy whispered to the others in his booth.

Everyone snickered appreciatively.

Against her better judgment, Hilda moved closer. Calvin held a lottery ticket.

"Look at those digits," he said. "Then look at the ones in the paper."

Hilda bent over and squinted at the ticket. "Your thumb is over the numbers," she said. "How can I see if your thumb's in the way?"

"You're looking upside down. Come around here and read it right side up."

They weren't actually angry with one another. It was just the excitement. They were getting close to something wonderful and they wanted to raise their voices.

"All right," Hilda was saying. "Hold your horses."

After she came around the bar, she read the numbers again. Several times. And while she did, Calvin watched her face the way a child will look at a parent, awaiting a decision.

"Lord Jesus," Hilda cried in exactly the same way Calvin had just moments before.

"*Lord Jesus!*" They said it together and it came out like a chorus.

Now everyone was up and they clustered around Calvin, squeezing Hilda out of the way, except for the high school girls who watched developments from their booth. Everyone knew Calvin, even the men from the surveying company. It was like a joyful family reunion.

Calvin held the lottery ticket with such determination his thumb and finger ached. When someone reached for it, for a closer look, he couldn't help snatching it out of danger.

Nobody knew who said what, but there was a chaos of conversation.

"Holy shit!"

And "Lord Jesus."

"How much is it worth?"

"A million."

"You sure?"

"Holy shit!"

"Lord Jesus."

And so on.

Paul Symonds, who was in his late thirties and had a prosperous took to him, finally emerged from his office just off the kitchen, clutching everyone's paycheque in his hand. When he figured out what was going on, he hung back for a moment or two, unable to understand a powerful envy that cascaded into his heart. He waited fruitlessly for it to turn out to be a mistake, not yet ready to accept that Calvin Smith, his tenant in the dingy apartment upstairs, was now a very rich man. Calvin Smith a millionaire? It seemed an act of trespassing, a betrayal of right and wrong.

There was still a lot of babbling going on, harmless little arguments.

"If it was me, I'd start spending right now, right this goddamned minute."

"No way. Better to plan it out. Sit down and get organized."

"Fuck that. I wouldn't even wait until I had the cheque."

"Shit, you're a bloody fool. I'd wanna see the cheque. Just in case."

And so on.

Randy Carstairs and Johnny Stephens did most of the talking and felt most of the excitement. They had insinuated themselves into the middle of the fray. They were so close to Calvin they touched him, a touching which had its own exotic excitement, like being first in line to witness the next miracle.

"You should celebrate, Cal," Randy said. "You should do something. Right this minute."

"Leave him alone," Johnny argued. "Let it sink in, for Christ's sake. Give the guy a break."

"C'mon, Cal. If you don't do something, you'll go crazy."

Calvin, though, had grown a little confused. Dozens of thoughts scurried through the tunnels in his mind, bumping into one another and falling down, then getting up again. It took several minutes of concentration before he found the will to act, a way that he could splurge.

"Coffee for everyone," he shouted. "Hilda, the coffee's on me."

Although some people had consumed their share of a small pond of free coffee already, no one really gave it much thought. There was simply too much excitement. Even Hilda, who kept sniffling with her cold, knew only how to grin.

Her boss found the will to speak. "Hilda, the man wants coffee all around."

"Yeah, sure," she said. "Comin' up."

That ended the hubbub of debate. Everyone gazed at Symonds, surprised that he had materialized at last. Now, at least, there was a spokesman, someone in authority who would know what to say. After all,

Symonds was a Rotarian. The employees of *Moravia's F ne Italian Foods* waited in anticipation.

"Calvin?" Symonds said, rising to the challenge. "Let me be the first one to congratulate you. I want to be the first to shake your hand."

"Lord Jesus," Calvin murmured, as if, only at this moment, with Paul Symonds wanting to shake his hand, his good fortune was actually real.

When Calvin reached out for the handshake, Symonds transferred the paycheques from his right hand to his left, then firmly did his duty.

There was enthusiastic applause.

Calvin, partially toothless, grinned from ear to ear, and it looked for all the world like a jagged fissure on the face of a cliff.

His job done, Symonds turned to his employees. "I have your cheques," he said, moving forward to hand them out.

People slipped away from Calvin, Hilda to pour twenty coffees, others to collect their cheques, Symonds to read the names. Only Randy and Johnny remained nearby, still touching the man who had been blessed by God, still full of ideas and suggestions.

"The first thing," Johnny said, "is to go up to the drugstore and check the ticket. The numbers are on the wall. That's the first thing."

"C'mon, Man," Randy countered. "It's right there in the newspaper, for Christ's sake."

"No, listen. That's what you've got to do. Make sure

of everything. I'll bet it's in the computer. I'll bet, if they feed it to the machine, it'll go off like a fucking siren."

Randy began to grin. "Yeah," he said. "Yeah."

"Whaddyuh say, Cal? Let's go up to the drugstore and blow their minds."

"Lord Jesus," Calvin said, although he was tiring now, finding it all too much to handle.

"We'll go with you. Right, Randy? We wanna see it."

They helped him up from the bar stool, without waiting for his reply. Calvin went along meekly and the three of them headed for the door.

"I've got your cheques, boys," Symonds said.

"We'll get 'em in a few minutes, as soon as we get back," Randy replied, hardly glancing over his shoulder.

They went outside into the cold.

THE TWO YOUNG MEN HELPED CALVIN up the street. It was less than a block but the sidewalks were slippery. They walked on either side of him, holding his arms, an awkward rhythm to their gait, the imbalance in the gap between their ages. Randy and Johnny wanted to hurry but Calvin was old and stiff. And he'd grown restive, considering he was a millionaire. When his companions decided to cut across the street, Calvin pulled them back, insisting they go to the stoplights where they could cross when the signal turned green.

They caused quite a stir at the drugstore. It was as if their unexplained euphoria was infectious. People grinned at them as they stumbled through the aisles, then laughed when Randy or Johnny laughed.

"C'mon, Cal," Randy urged.

The old man was practically carried, puffing and snorting from the cold and their excitement, across the floor towards the counter where the final verification awaited them. Cal had brought the newspaper from the restaurant, although he had not realized he had until he dropped it as they approached the counter. Randy laughed and stooped to pick it up.

"Here, Cal," he said. "Hold onto it. It's a souvenir now, my man."

The girl behind the counter, mystified by their behavior, regarded them with tired disdain. She chewed a large wad of gum with a vicious intensity, bludgeoning it with jackhammer jaws. She stopped abruptly, though, as Cal and his friends approached. The gum just loitered in her mouth, waiting for the punishment that inevitably would resume.

The girl stood behind the counter, rudely silent.

At first the men were incoherent. The best they could manage was a series of wheezes, their laughter and words cut off by breathlessness, which tried her patience even more.

"Yes?" she said at last.

"Cal," Randy gasped. "Give her the ticket."

Calvin glanced at him in wonder.

"Cal. The ticket, for Christ's sake."

There was a brief, but terrifying moment in which, simultaneously, all three of them feared the ticket was lost. But at last Calvin produced it from his jacket pocket and the girl, with some trepidation, took it from his hand.

"You want me to check it?"

"Jesus," Randy said. "Of course we want you to check it."

The girl began to beat the gum again, really put out this time. She turned to some printouts on the wall and ran a fingernail painted a bright Chinese red down the list of numbers.

Anticipating the result, Johnny gleefully winked at Randy and elbowed Calvin in the ribs.

Bored, the girl turned back to the waiting men. "Not a winner," she said in a rushing monotone.

"*What*?"

"Not a winner," the girl repeated with some exasperation.

"Whaddyuh mean, 'not a winner?'" Johnny sputtered.

"It isn't a winning ticket. Okay?"

Randy simply stared. He gazed at the girl and then he stared at Calvin. Calvin gazed back at him but there was nothing notable in the look. He just grinned his jagged grin and didn't seem to understand.

For a moment, Johnny was furious. The girl had made a mistake. Roughly, he snatched the newspaper from under Calvin's arm.

"Look at this, for Christ's sake. Look." He thrust the newspaper at the girl with such vehemence, she took a step backwards. "Compare the numbers. You think we're crazy. Calvin, here, just won the whole bundle."

The girl took the newspaper but held it at arm's length, as if it already had been used for wrapping fish.

"C'mon. Look at it."

At last, she compared the numbers on the ticket with those published by the newspaper.

"See?" Johnny said. "They're the same numbers."

The girl nodded and attacked her gum again. Johnny glanced at Randy. His face kept changing color, from red to white to red again. Calvin continued to wheeze, each breath a cry of pain.

"I don't get it" the girl murmured.

"Check your list again. Maybe you screwed up."

She pulled the newspaper closer, almost touching it with her nose. Finally, an eternity later, she raised baleful eyes to Johnny.

"It's a joke," she said.

"Whaddyuh mean 'a joke?'"

"Someone's changed a number. Here in the newspaper."

"*What*? Lemme see."

The girl put the newspaper on the counter and smoothed it with her hand, the way she might iron a blouse or a dress.

"See? Someone's turned the one into a seven."

"Where?"

"Right here." And she brought a blinding fingernail down on the second number from the right. "Black pen. The ticket doesn't win anything."

As if they were connected to one another, the three

men studied the newspaper. Calvin couldn't see anything but Randy and Johnny could. Someone with a black pen and a lot of patience had altered the number all right. Now that it had been pointed out, it was there as plain as day.

"Shit," Johnny murmured.

"Sorry," the girl whispered.

But there was no condolence powerful enough. The three men turned away and headed for the door, silent in their loss.

Outside, they zipped up their jackets and Calvin buttoned the charcoal sports coat he would now have to keep forever. The street was brilliant with an ironic sunshine and people moved to and fro, the way they always did. The three companions, lost in this sameness, could not look at one another. Instead, they stood outside the door a time, trying to digest their loss of luck. Like sour milk, it did not go down well.

"You win some and you lose some," Calvin said finally, purely to have something to say.

Together, Johnny and Randy nodded.

At last they began the long walk back towards *Moravia's F ne Italian Foods*. On the way, much to his shame and surprise, not really understanding why, Johnny began to weep. Whether it was his disappointment or because Calvin seemed almost relieved, he would have been hard-pressed to say.

BY THE TIME THEY GOT BACK to the restaurant, the four high school girls and the two men from the surveying company had left. But everyone else was there. They'd had time to get to the bank and they were back, anticipating Calvin's return. Even Paul Symonds had hung around, stationing himself behind the cash register. Loudly, Happy Hilda cleared a table near the back.

There was no need for an explanation. Calvin was no longer a millionaire. It was etched upon his face. Eventually people came forward and Johnny and Randy explained what had happened. There were awkward little gestures of understanding and consolation, pats on the arm, shrugs of sympathy, grunts of empathy.

Finally, after it was all straightened out and everyone knew what had happened, the group began to disperse. Calvin retreated first. It was five or six steps through the snow to the doorway to the stairs which led to his second floor apartment. He moved to leave the restaurant.

Then Symonds got in on the act.

"What about those coffees, Cal?"

Calvin turned, puzzled, not remembering at first the round he had bought the house during that brief, ecstatic time he had been rich.

"The bill's ten-fifty."

Calvin's withered forehead grew deeper furrows of worry. "I haven't got it," he said.

In silence, Symonds glared at the shrinking man.

"Can I owe you 'til my pension cheque comes in?"

"Doesn't look like I have any choice," Symonds said after a pointed hesitation.

Johnny and Randy and the others stared at the aging

carpet under their feet. They felt an intense embarrassment. It didn't quite manage to be anger.

Symonds came out from behind the cash and gave Randy and Johnny their cheques. At that point, everyone began to calm down and things became typical again. There's a comfort in finding your spot and staying there once more. For Randy and Johnny, it was too late to go to the bank. With private inner shrugs, they accepted the fact they would be broke for another day.

As it turned out, before the others left, they divvied up Calvin's bill and paid Symonds what was owed.

After that, in every way, things returned to normal.

Barry Grills

EPILOGUE

I HAVE LONG BEEN AN ADMIRER of the short story form in writing. I believe Canadians are especially adept at them. Our Nobel Prize in Literature recipient, Alice Munro, is a case in point.

For me, at the beginning of my career, the writing of a short story had the advantage of requiring only a few days or weeks to write, edit, rewrite, etc. The writing of novels is measured in years. But a novel gives one room. More than the short story, in my opinion, it provides richer opportunities for characters to become the protagonists they seem to need to be.

Writers do not get to pick which genre or form will make them most comfortable. I tend to believe the genre or form picks *us*. Our ideas pick *us*. Our themes and perceptions about people, issues, times and events pick *us*. Writers are not merely vessels—I don't mean it that way—but if we are letting the work pour out of us unrestrained (for later editing), it is in *that* sense that what makes us comfortable picks *us*.

I'm still writing. Even as an old-timer, I have more novels in process. And I am always open to having a brand new one pick *me*. But I don't think in short stories any longer and I would be dismayed if I ever contemplated writing another. They were an appropriate form for me to begin writing fiction.

I wonder, though, about my Grade Nine English teacher, Miss Phillips. I wonder how she arrived at the conclusion—before I ever contemplated it—that I might potentially live my life primarily as a writer. It's a mystery. Unfortunately, many mysteries are never really solved. And the mystery itself becomes its own secret pleasure.

And I enjoy a good mystery as much as the next person.

COCK-EYED VOICE: STORIES

ABOUT THE AUTHOR

Barry Grills is a former chair of The Writers' Union of Canada and the Book and Periodical Council. His short stories have appeared in various literary magazines and anthologies, including *Best Canadian Stories*. His critically acclaimed memoir, *Every Wolf's Howl*, won an Alberta Book Award for its publisher, Freehand Books. His first Fluid Grouse Enterprises book, *Roadkill*, was a finalist in both the Next Generation Indie Book Awards and the Whistler Independent Book Awards. He is also the author of three musical biographies on the lives and careers of Anne Murray, Alanis Morissette and Céline Dion. His work on an updated version of Dion's life, co-authored with Jim Brown, was the source for a CBC television movie. He currently lives and works in North Bay, Ontario, Canada.